Discovering Literature Series

CHALLENGING LEVEL

D1397690

The Hobbit

~or~

There and Back Again

A Teaching Guide

by Mary Elizabeth

Illustrations by Kathy Kifer

Journey Strand

Dedicated to
Marjorie Y. Lipson

The Hobbit
Published by:
Ballantine Books
Ballantine Mail Sales
400 Hahn Road
Westminster, MD 21157
1 (800) 733-3000

Teaching Guide Published by:
Garlic Press
605 Powers
Eugene, OR 97402

ISBN 0-931993-90-3
Order Number GP-090

www.garlicpress.com

Table of Contents

Table of Contents, Cont.

NOTES TO THE TEACHER

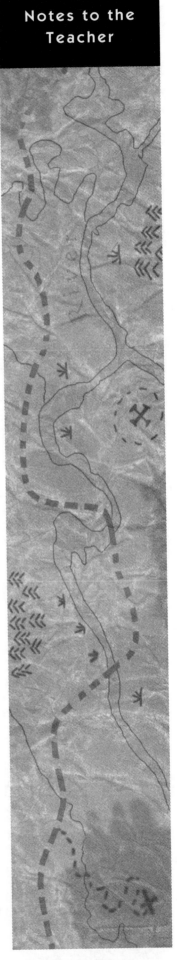

The Discovering Literature Series is designed to develop a student's appreciation for good literature, to improve reading comprehension, and to introduce students to the techniques of literary criticism that reflect our best understanding of how to make meaning from texts. At the Challenging Level, we focus on a variety of reading strategies that can help students construct meaning from their experience with literature as well as make connections between their reading and the rest of their lives. The strategies reflect the demands of each literature selection. In this study guide, we will focus on beginning a book, plot, setting and mood, characterization, rhetoric, maps and runes, point of view, fantasy, foreshadowing and flashback, irony, parody, theme, and the hero's journey.

ORGANIZATION OF THIS LITERATURE GUIDE

The following discussion explains the various elements that structure the series at the Challenging Level.

Each chapter analysis is organized into three basic elements: **Journal and Discussion Topics, Chapter Vocabulary,** and **Chapter Summary.** One or more of the Journal and Discussion Topics and all of the Chapter Vocabulary can either be displayed on the board or on an overhead projector before each chapter is read. The selected Journal and Discussion Topics will help to focus the students' reading of the chapter. Choose questions that will not give away important plot elements. Introducing the Chapter Vocabulary prior to students' reading insures that their reading is not disrupted by the frequent need to look up a word. Guide students in using one of the vocabulary exercises from page 6 to preview the Chapter Vocabulary.

Journal and Discussion Topics

The **Journal and Discussion Topics** include directions for the students' **Reader Response Journals** and questions for **Discussion** will help the students become engaged with the literature. Students will benefit by reading with their journals beside them. This will allow them to easily note any unfamiliar vocabulary that was not presented to the class, questions they have about the literature, and their own reactions as they enter into the experience of the story. Journals can also be used for written dialogue between you and students. If you wish to do this, periodically collect the journals and respond to students' comments. It is important for students to know beforehand whether their journals are private or public. In either case, journals should not be corrected or graded, but only recorded for being used. You may also wish to keep your own journal.

Discussion can take place between partners, in small groups, or as a whole class. Students may also wish to reflect on the discussion in their journals. Discussion starters include:

1. A group retelling of the chapter in which everyone participates.
2. Each group member telling the most striking moment in the chapter for him or her.
3. Each group member sharing a question she or he would like to ask the author or a character about the chapter.
4. Each student telling what he or she liked most or least about the chapter.

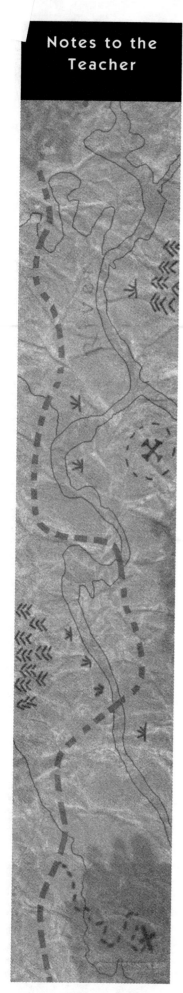

5. A discussion of how the chapter relates to the preceding chapter and the rest of the book that preceded it.

Discussion can end with predictions about what will happen in the next chapter. Each student should note predictions in her or his journal.

Always ask students to retell (or summarize) the material. The retelling can be oral, artistic (for example, a storyboard), or prose. Retelling can take place in the discussion groups or in the journals.

Chapter Vocabulary

The **Chapter Vocabulary** includes definitions of key words from each chapter. To save time, students need only to copy, not look up, definitions. The more meaningful vocabulary exercises are, the more easily students will retain vocabulary. Suggestions for teaching vocabulary:

1. Finding relationships between and among words helps students learn the words better than treating them separately. Have students create a web or other graphic, showing the relationships between and among the vocabulary words. Encourage them to add other related words to their web.

2. A group of words that primarily includes nouns can be used to label a picture. For example, for Chapter 3, you might provide a landscape picture and have students label gullies, ravines, and bogs.

3. Have students use the words in a piece of writing, for example a poem, a one-act play, or a diary entry written from the point of view of one of the characters.

4. Have students research the etymology of the vocabulary words and keep notes on their findings.

5. Have students make and exchange crossword puzzles made with the vocabulary words.

6. Have students write and exchange a **cloze exercise** using the vocabulary words. A cloze exercise has a blank for each vocabulary word, and the surrounding context must clearly indicate which word belongs in each blank.

Chapter Summary

The **Chapter Summary** for each chapter is included for teacher use. It provides an at-a-glance scan of the chapter events and should be used as a companion to the work of literature being studied, not instead of it. Use it to refresh your memory about the contents of each chapter.

The Groupings of Literature

We have among our titles a group of works that could be presented as part of a unit called "The Journey." We present groupings of literature so that you can easily present works as a unit. The works of literature resonate with each other, providing a multi-faceted look at a variety of **themes** such as:

- The journey as a metaphor
- Coping with change
- Safety versus risk-taking
- Change is opportunity (a Chinese saying)
- Choices
- Trust
- Flexibility
- The journey versus the arrival
- Resourcefulness

Since no substantial work of literature has only a single theme, "The Journey" is not the only possible grouping for the works of literature. But references to themes can both help focus students' attention as they read and help them link works of literature together in meaningful ways. A grouping of books can also throw light on **Big Ideas.** Big Ideas worth considering include the following:

- How does context (cultural, social, etc.) affect us?
- How can personal desire be balanced with other responsibilities?
- What kinds of circumstances lead to personal development and growth?
- How is place important in our lives? What kinds of changes can occur when we change our location?

OTHER FEATURES OF THE CHALLENGING LEVEL

Strategy Pages

Strategy Pages throughout the series have been developed to increase students' understanding of strategies they can use to enhance their understanding of literature. Some important examples are:

- Monitoring (such as adjusting reading rate; using context, including illustrations, to clarify meaning; rereading; etc.)
- Identifying important information (such as marking a text)
- Summarizing
- Evaluating
- Understanding the tools that writers use to make meaning—the elements of literature such as theme, plot, character, allusion, symbolism, metaphor, etc.

The pages for each literature selection reinforce the strategies important for engaging deeply with that particular work of literature. You may copy and distribute these pages. Students can answer on the back of the page or on a separate sheet of paper.

Testing

At the end of each chapter grouping, a comprehensive open-book **Test** has been provided for your use. Each test includes vocabulary exercises and short essays. You may copy and distribute these pages.

An Answer Key is provided at the back of the book for each Test. Answers to essay questions are, of necessity, incomplete and only suggestive. Students' answers should be fully developed.

Writer's Forum

Suggestions for writing are presented under the **Writer's Forum** heading throughout this guide. You can choose from these suggestions or substitute your own creative-writing ideas.

Each Writer's Forum includes both instruction and directions for a particular writing task. Students will write in a variety of genres relating to the text and their own experience of the text. As you plan writing lessons, allow enough time for students to engage in the writing process:

- **Prewrite** (brainstorm and plan their work)
- **Draft** (give a shape to their ideas on paper)
- **Review** (revisit their work with an eye to improving it, on their own as well as with peers, with you, or with others)
- **Revise** (make changes that they feel will improve their draft)
- **Proofread** (check for accuracy in grammar, mechanics, and spelling)
- **Publish** (present their work to others in some way)

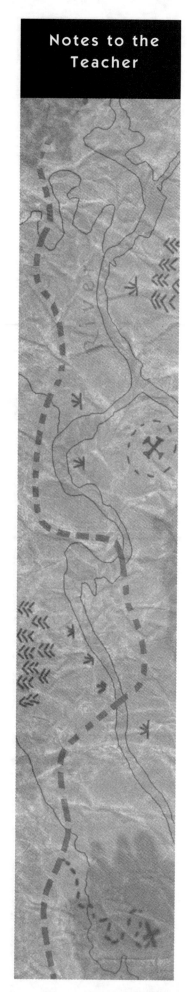

INTRODUCING THE LITERATURE

Students will be better prepared to become involved with the work of literature if they can place it in a context. The process of **contextualizing** a work of literature begins with accessing their **prior knowledge** about the book, the author, the genre, and the subject. A class discussion is a good forum for this to take place. After you have found out what, if any, familiarity students have with the book and author and what they have been able to discern about the genre and subject, you can provide any necessary background knowledge and, if it seems appropriate, correct any misapprehensions students have. See **Strategy 1: Beginning a Book,** pages 10–11.

Explain that in a work of fiction, an author creates an imaginary world. An important task in beginning a literature selection is to come to terms with that world. Point out that it is possible to consciously assess one's own understanding of literature and that this process is called **metacognitive reflection.** You may wish to model this process using a **think-aloud** approach as you go through the material on pages 10–11. To do this, simply read aloud the portion of *The Hobbit* needed to answer the questions, and speak aloud your thoughts as you formulate your responses, making explicit the connections and prior knowledge you are developing in your thoughts.

After students have a beginning notion of the context of a work, you can proceed with the prereading activities that students will do prior to reading every chapter.

Sample Lesson Plan

Engaging **Prereading** activities include the following:

- Preview vocabulary and do a vocabulary exercise.
- Review the events of the previous chapter.
- Based on what they already know, have students examine their expectations about what will happen next, but be ready for surprises. Have students consider the chapter title and any illustrations. Use appropriate questions from page 11 or a prediction guide. Students can fill in the guide as a class, in groups, or individually. Encourage students to continue using this kind of self-questioning in their Reader-Response Journals.

During Reading, students read with their Reader Response Journals. (You may wish to give them some of the journal and discussion topics before they read, or after they have read a particular portion of the book.) Additional journal activities they can use with every chapter include the following:

- A summary of the events of the chapter
- Evaluations of the characters and/or text
- Questions about what they have read
- Associations they have made between the text and other texts, experiences, or situations
- Notes on the images the text evoked
- Notes on the feelings the text evoked

After Reading, students complete the Journal and Discussion Topics, the Writer's Forum and Strategy Pages (if any), and the Test.

TOLKIEN AND SPECIES

In *The Hobbit*, sometimes the names of Middle-earth species (such as elves and men) are capitalized and sometimes not. We will always present them in lower case.

Bibliography

As you and your students immerse yourselves in this work of literature, you may wish to consult other works by the same author, thematically related works, video and/or audio productions of the work, and criticism. Here is a brief list of works that may be useful:

Adams, Richard. *Watership Down.* 1974.

Alexander, Lloyd. *The Arkadians.* 1995.

Alexander, Lloyd. *The Book of Three.* 1964.

Carpenter, Humphrey. *Tolkien: A Biography.* (Ballantine Books: New York, 1977)

Carpenter, Humphrey, ed. *The Letters of J. R. R. Tolkien.* (Houghton Mifflin Company: Boston, 1981)

Cooper, Susan. *Over Sea, Under Stone.* 1965.

Green, William H. *The Hobbit: A Journey into Maturity.* (Twayne: New York, 1995)

Homer. *The Odyssey.* (many translations available)

Jacques, Brian. *Redwall.* 1986.

Le Guin, Ursula. *A Wizard of Earthsea.* 1968.

Tolkien, J. R. R. *The Annotated Hobbit.* (Houghton Mifflin: Boston, 1988)

Tolkien, J. R. R. *Farmer Giles of Ham.* (Houghton Mifflin: Boston, 1978)

Tolkien, J. R. R. *J. R. R. Tolkien Soundbook* (Caedmon, New York, 1977

Tolkien, J. R. R. *Smith of Wootton Major* (Houghton Mifflin: Boston, 1978)

Tolkien, J. R. R. *The Lord of the Rings* (three part series):
   The Fellowship of the Ring (Ballantine Books, New York, 1955, 1965, 1982)
   The Two Towers (Ballantine Books, New York, 1955, 1965, 1982)
   The Return of the King (Ballantine Books, New York, 1955, 1965, 1983)

Tolkien, J. R. R. *The Silmarillion.* (Houghton Mifflin Company: Boston, 1977)

Tolkien, J. R. R. *The Tolkien Reader.* (Ballantine Books: New York, 1966)

Tolkien, J. R. R. *Unfinished Tales of Númenor and Middle-earth.* (Houghton Mifflin Co.: Boston, 1980)

Tyler, J. E. A. *The Tolkien Companion.* (St. Martin's Press: New York, 1976)

White, T. H. *The Sword in the Stone.* 1958.

Pronunciation Guides for proper nouns in *The Hobbit* may be found in *The Silmarillion,* pages 310–311, and in *The Return of the King,* pages 487–492.

Note: You may wish to inform students that British spelling is used in *The Hobbit.* Hence, they sometimes will find words spelled with an *ou* which we spell in American English with just an *o* (neighbourhood, colours, parlour, favourite, honour, clamour) and double *ll's* where they might expect a single one (counsellor, travelling). The trolls speak in a lower-class dialect.

Strategy 1 Beginning a Book

Directions: Read the explanation, then answer the questions.

When an artist or craftworker sets about creating a work, there are a set of standard tools, techniques, and products available. The painter, for example, has brushes of various shapes and sizes, canvas of various descriptions, and a choice of oil paints, watercolors, acrylics, tempera, etc. The product may be a portrait, a still-life, a landscape, or an abstract work. And the techniques used may include various kinds of brush strokes, pen and ink, wash, spattering, etc. In addition, there are certain conventions, such as perspective, that the painter may choose to employ or not. The painter does not use every technique and material in every painting, and the painter's choices are guided by the painter's goal, which might be the answer to a question such as, "How can I effectively communicate my vision?" The viewer coming to see the finished product can see it all at one time. Moving closer and further away, attending to detail, shape, color, texture, and the effect of the whole, the viewer can come to understand the painting.

The writer is an artist who works in words which create images, thoughts, and feelings in the reader. Like the painter, the writer usually isn't there when the reader experiences the product (in this case a book), but reading is, nevertheless, an act of communication. Like the painter, the writer works to communicate a vision to people who are not present with him or her. The reader's understanding of the standard tools, techniques, products, and conventions of the writer help the reader to understand the vision. But at the same time that we try to understand the writer's communication, we must acknowledge that each reader also brings an individual and unique understanding to the act of reading, and so no two readers will experience a book in exactly the same way. Different readers will have different insights and feelings, so discussion between and among readers can enrich the experience of all.

Beginning a book is particularly important, because readers starting a book are entering a new and uncharted territory. When you are starting a book, paying particular attention to the writer's use of tools, techniques, and conventions can help.

TITLE: It is a convention for a novel to have a title, found on the front cover, the spine, and the title page. The title of the book may explicitly tell what the book is about, may hint about the story, or may seem very mysterious. Depending on the title, you may feel interested, curious, hopeful, etc. Sometimes a book has a subtitle—a second part of the title written below the main title. Often, the subtitle appears only on the title page. The author's name follows immediately after the title. If you know anything about the author already, for example, that Tolkien was a philologist and studied medieval literature, it might help you make predictions about the content of the book.

COVER ILLUSTRATION: Most books have a picture on the cover. The writer may or may not have had a voice in what appears, so the illustration may not represent the writer's vision. Nevertheless, it can give you some idea of characters, setting, and plot in the story.

COPYRIGHT PAGE: The copyright page tells the dates of the book's publication. It can help you know whether the book is recent or older.

OTHER BOOKS BY: Sometimes there is a list that names other books by the same author. If you are familiar with any of these other works, you

Beginning a Book, cont.

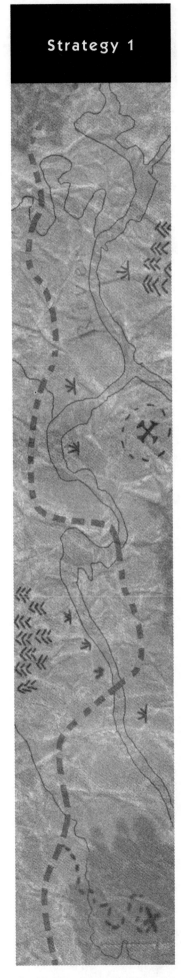

may have some idea of what is to come. This is also true if you have heard about the book from friends, read a book review, heard the book on audiotape, or seen a movie version. This is some of your prior knowledge about the book.

TABLE OF CONTENTS: While some books have unnamed divisions, sometimes authors title their chapters. Like the book title, these chapter titles may reveal more or less about what happens in the book.

INSIDE ILLUSTRATIONS: Some books are illustrated throughout with drawings, paintings, photographs, etc. This book is not, but there are two maps. See page 20 for more information about them.

BACK COVER BLURB: The note on the back cover is advertising, meant to give away enough of the story to pique your interest and convince you to buy the book. It doesn't necessarily reflect the writer's vision or the most meaningful view of the story. In addition, it often tells you about an important part in the middle of the story, and you may prefer not to know this in advance.

FIRST FEW PARAGRAPHS: The first few paragraphs of the story provide the writer with the first opportunity to introduce the characters, plot, setting, and theme of the story. Read carefully to learn as much as you can about the world of the book.

1. What is your reaction to the title of the book?

2. Based on the title, what do you think this book will be about?

3. Describe the cover illustration. What can you gather from it?

4. How long has it been since this book was first published?

5. What, if anything, do you already know about Tolkien, his works, or *The Hobbit*?

6. What can you tell about the story from the chapter titles?

7. How do the chapter titles seem to relate to the title of the whole?

8. What chapter might the cover illustration come from?

9. Read to the middle of page three. What does the narrator indicate is the reader's role in reading?

10. What is the narrator like? Can you trust the narrator's perceptions? How did you decide?

11. Who seem(s) to be the most important character(s)? How can you tell?

12. Where does the story take place? Is it a real setting or a setting created by the author? What special characteristics does the setting have?

13. What clues are there to the genre of this story?

14. What does the theme or focus of the story seem to be?

15. What do you predict will happen next in the story?

16. What more do you want to know about the setting and the characters?

Chapter 1

"An Unexpected Party"

Journal and Discussion Topics

1. Now that you've read the first chapter, what do you think the story will be about? What evidence supports your conclusion?
2. What is Bilbo going to say at the top of page 6 before he interrupts himself? How do you know? What conclusions can you draw?
3. Why aren't the dwarves in possession of their treasure? How does this make them feel?
4. How does the dwarves' music affect Bilbo?
5. Gandalf says Bilbo is "as fierce as a dragon in a pinch." What evidence is there for or against this claim? Why does Gandalf say this?
6. Why does Gandalf choose Bilbo? How can Gandalf's word make Bilbo a burglar? How can Gandalf know things about Bilbo that Bilbo doesn't even know?
7. Does Thorin have faith in Bilbo? How can you tell?
8. Do you think Bilbo will go with the dwarves? Why or why not? Would you? Why or why not?
9. What in this chapter is realistic or possible in our world?
10. What in this chapter is imaginary or impossible in our world?
11. In your own words, tell the important events of this chapter in a sequence that makes sense to you.

Vocabulary

laburnum: 5, small yellow-flowered shrub
prosy: 5, lacking imagination
scuttled: 6, ran a short distance swiftly
flustered: 6, upset
throng: 8, a crowd
depredations: 9, laying waste
haughty: 10, proud
larders: 11, places where food is stored
flummoxed: 11, confused
confusticate: 11, confuse (made up word)
bebother: 11, thoroughly annoy
ere: 14, before
yore: 14, a long time ago
hoard: 14, a hidden supply of something
wrought: 14, made using art

delves: 14, digs
conspirator: 16, one who schemes secretly
audacious: 16, bold, daring, rash
ingenious: 16, clever
estimable: 16, worthy of esteem or respect
descendant: 17, family member born later
reviving: 17, recovering
expedition: 18, a journey with a purpose
parchment: 19, animal skin for writing
obstinately: 22, stubbornly
prudent: 22, having wisdom and judgment
remuneration: 22, pay for service
plunder: 23, stolen goods
Necromancer: 25, sorcerer
witless: 25, having lost the ability to think

Summary

Bilbo Baggins, a well-to-do Hobbit of Hobbiton in Middle-earth, is visited by Gandalf, a wandering wizard. Gandalf invites Bilbo to share an adventure. Bilbo refuses , but it is clear that one part of Bilbo is captivated by the idea of travel and adventure. Bilbo invites Gandalf to tea the following day, but only to get rid of him. Unbeknownst to Bilbo, Gandalf makes a magic sign on Bilbo's front door, and Bilbo is quite shocked the next day when 13 dwarves led by Thorin Oakenshield, as well as Gandalf, arrive for tea. The dwarves reveal that they are on a quest to recover their treasure, captured years before by a fierce dragon. Gandalf has, for reasons of his own, chosen Bilbo as the burglar for the dwarves' expedition. Bilbo at first refuses outright, but he is gradually tempted to enter the discussion. He has not definitely committed himself to the adventure by the time the dwarves retire for the night.

Strategy 2 Plot—The Design of a Story

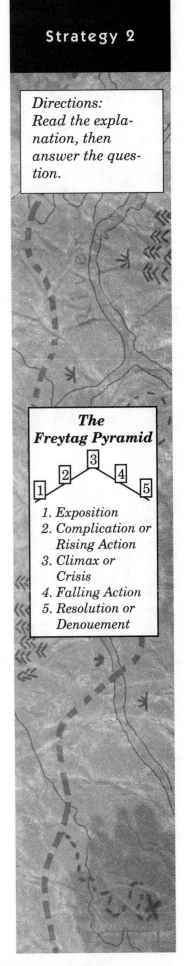

There are exciting stories and dull stories. There are westerns, adventure stories, mysteries, romances, thrillers, horror stories, science fiction stories, and fantasies. There are stories with happy endings and stories with sad endings. These differences can make stories seem worlds apart. But there is a common set of characteristics that almost all stories have—whether they are long or short, for adults or young people—that make them stories.

Every story has a plot or sequence of actions, a setting or settings where the action takes place, a character or group of characters who take action, and a narrator who tells the story to the reader.

People who study literature have come up with several different ways of talking about plot. When people talk about stories with young children, they often refer to the beginning, the middle, and the end. This is not just a notion for small children. These three parts are the way screenwriters and television writers arrange their scripts. Dramatists, on the other hand, often work with a 5-act play. The 5 acts each represents an essential and sequential part of the drama. Narrative is also often presented in high school and college classes as having a 5-part structure as follows:

1. **Exposition:** introduction of essential background information, as well as characters, situations, and conflicts. Exposition may be found throughout a story, as well as at the beginning.
2. **Complication or Rising Action:** the beginning of the central conflict in the story.
3. **Crisis:** (sometimes called the **turning point**) usually the point at which the main character's action or choice determines the outcome of the conflict. Or, **Climax:** the high point of the action.
4. **Falling Action:** the time when all the pieces fall into place and the ending becomes inevitable.
5. **Resolution or Denouement:** the conflicts are resolved and the story is concluded.

The Freytag Pyramid

1. *Exposition*
2. *Complication or Rising Action*
3. *Climax or Crisis*
4. *Falling Action*
5. *Resolution or Denouement*

So do we look at a story as having 5 parts or 3 parts? One way we can think about it is to see where the 5 parts fit into the beginning, middle and end:

> **Beginning:** Exposition
> **Middle:** Complication, ending with the Crisis
> **End:** Climax (the beginning of the end) and Resolution

Writers adapt the plot structure to a particular story. They decide how much exposition should be included and where, how many conflicts there are; what's told to the reader; and what is left for the reader to figure out.

1. As you read *The Hobbit*, pause at the end of each chapter, and identify for yourself where it fits in the plot structure. Place it on a Freytag Pyramid of your own. Note the places in the story where you find the beginning of each of the five parts. The shape of your pyramid may not exactly match the model in the margin.

old forest
—road

the shire

wilderland

misty
mountains

Chapter 2

"Roast Mutton"

Journal and Discussion Topics

1. Sometimes in literature a change of clothing is symbolic of a new role. What do you think Bilbo's change of apparel might mean?
2. How does life on the trail differ from the life Bilbo is accustomed to? How does he cope?
3. Why do you think it is significant that people in the area in which they camp haven't heard of the king?
4. What saves the dwarves from the trolls?
5. How do the others react to Bilbo's mention of the key?
6. Compare and contrast the speech of the dwarves and the speech of the trolls.
7. How do you imagine the trolls look? Draw a picture.
8. What does Bilbo argue about with himself when he sees the trolls?
9. What do you think of the dwarves' ability to make strategic plans? Give evidence.
10. In this chapter, what important help does Bilbo provide toward attaining the dwarves' goal?
11. Think of another book in which somebody got out of a tight situation by a trick rather than by violence. Compare and contrast this with the situation in this chapter.

Vocabulary

defrayed: 29, paid for expenses
esteemed: 29, honored
requisite: 29, necessary
punctual: 29, on time
paraphernalia: 30, equipment
laden: 30, carrying a load
bolted: 33, ran away
canny: 34, safe
cavalcade: 34, procession
toothsome: 35, attractive
purloined: 36, stolen

copped: 36, caught
throttled: 36, strangled
blighter: 37, fellow, guy
lout: 37, a cruel person
bickering: 41, quarreling
incantations: 42, magic spells
scabbard: 43, a sheath for a sword
hilts: 43, handles
smith: 43, one who works with metals
embers: 43, glowing ashes of a fire
waylaid: 44, ambushed

Summary

Upon awakening the next morning, Bilbo believes that the dwarves have left on their expedition. He is both relieved and disappointed. Gandalf arrives and sends him scurrying off to the meeting place without any chance to pack, and he is just in time to join the dwarves. As the troupe passes beyond hobbit-lands into less populated areas with dreary landscape, the weather begins to turn bad and Gandalf disappears without warning.

They are caught in a cold rain and unable to light a fire when their lookout spies a light in the distance. They decide to approach the light and send Bilbo-the-burglar to investigate. Bilbo discovers three trolls sitting around a fire and is soon caught trying to pick one of their pockets. The trolls fight about Bilbo, and he manages to elude them by hiding behind a tree. But the dwarves, hearing a commotion, come hurrying up and are caught one by one and popped into sacks. As the trolls are about to eat them, Gandalf returns. By throwing his voice, he tricks the trolls into fighting among themselves until the sun comes up and turns them to stone. After raiding the trolls' cave for food and treasure—notably several swords made for the goblin wars and a dagger for Bilbo—the band sets out again.

Strategy 3   Setting and Mood

Directions: Read the explanation, then answer the question.

Setting is both the world in which the story takes place and the changing scenery that serves as the backdrop for each scene or chapter. Setting includes what the characters see, hear, smell, and can touch in their environment. Sights include:

- Time of day
- Season of the year
- Plants and animals
- Natural features
- Weather
- Landscape
- Buildings or other structures

The general setting of this story is Middle-earth, a land with certain kinds of people; certain kinds of landscape; certain plants, animals, and weather; and certain rules and customs. The particular setting within Middle-earth changes from scene to scene and chapter to chapter.

Some parts of a setting come from nature, and some are made by the creatures of the world in which the story takes place. The first part of the setting described in this book is Bilbo's hobbit hole, built by his father, and furnished by Bilbo himself. The setting described on pages 32–33, the night they encountered the trolls, describes a natural setting.

Settings can serve different functions in different stories and at different times in the same story. It may be a mere backdrop to the story, or it may have a more integral part. The setting may be symbolic and be a source of information about the inhabitants of the area. The setting may create conflicts for the characters of the story. The setting may help or hinder the characters in achieving their goal. It may provide materials or resources that help the characters solve problems, or create physical hardships or challenges that are difficult to overcome. Setting also helps establish characterization (see **Strategy 4**, page 16). For example, from reading the description of Bilbo's hobbit hole on page 1, you can begin to get an idea of Bilbo's character, even before you know his name. The setting of a story affects how we and the characters feel about their surroundings. This feeling is called **mood**. The setting can make things seem pleasant, or give an air of foreboding that makes you think that something bad is about to happen.

Although a novel is classified as a narrative, that is, a type of writing that tells a story, sections of a novel that deal with the setting are usually passages of description.

As you notice the setting, try to figure out what the writer is trying to convey. Pay attention to the possibilities and problems created by the setting, and the mood the setting creates for you in order to take advantage of hints the writer is giving about what might happen next.

1. Extend the following chart to create a record of *The Hobbit* settings and their functions. Skim Chapters 1 and 2 and enter the settings you find. Then, continue the chart as you read farther.

Page #	Setting Description	Function(s) in Story

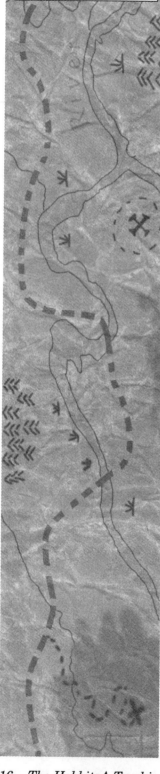

Strategy 4 Characterization

Directions:
Read the expla-
nation, then
answer the ques-
tions.

A **Character** in a story is someone or something whose actions, choices, thoughts, ideas, words, and influence are important in developing the plot. Characters are often people, but also include other living creatures, and sometimes even non-living things. A force, such as good or evil, can operate as a character in a story.

Most stories have a single character or a small group of characters whose goal or problem is the core of the plot. This character or group of characters is called the protagonist. The protagonist does not have to be good, but a good protagonist may be referred to as the "hero" of the story. Readers usually identify with the protagonist and hope that the protagonist will succeed in attaining his or her goal. The character, group, or force that opposes the protagonist is called the antagonist. In certain stories, this character may be referred to as the villain. (See Strategy 9, Plot Conflict, page 28.).

Characters, whether human or not, have what we call "personality"— a set of characteristic traits and features by which we recognize them. Personality is what helps us distinguish one dwarf from another dwarf, one troll from another troll. **Characterization** is the name for the techniques a writer uses to reveal the personality of characters to the reader. Characterization is achieved in a number of different ways:

- **Words:** comments by the narrator, dialogue by others about the character, as well as the character's own words; what is said, as well as how it is said—dialect, slang, and tone are important
- **Thoughts:** what's going on in the character's mind, the character's motives and choices
- **Appearance:** the character's physical characteristics and clothing (these may be symbolic; for example, Gandalf's white beard suggests wisdom)
- **Action:** what the character does
- **Interactions:** how the character relates to others
- **Names:** often symbolic of a major character trait or role
- **Chosen Setting:** the items, furnishings, etc., with which the character chooses to surround him- or herself
- **Change/Development:** the occurrence of and direction of change or development that a character undergoes inwardly

1. What techniques does Tolkien use to characterize the trolls?

2. What is the effect on you of the name "Bilbo Baggins"?

3. How does Thorin interact with others?

4. What changes in Bilbo's character have you seen so far in the story?

5. How would you characterize Gandalf and his role in the adventure so far?

Chapter 3

"A Short Rest"

Journal and Discussion Topics

1. An elf gives the company a choice of singing or eating. How do their reactions fit their characters? What would you have done? Why?
2. What coincidence helps the dwarves during their stay in Rivendell?
3. What does Elrond think of the dwarves? What would you say to him about this?
4. How does the stop in Rivendell help the dwarves move toward attaining their goal?

Vocabulary

homely: 46, like a home
gullies: 47, trenches or small valleys
ravines: 47, narrow, steep-sided valleys
bogs: 47, wet, poorly drained areas
slithered: 47, to slide like a snake
faggots: 48, bundles of sticks
bannocks: 48, flat bread
folly: 49, a foolish act
hark: 49, pay close attention
gruffly: 49, harshly, sternly, or brusquely

parapet: 50, a low wall around the edge
bridle: 50, the bit and reins for a horse
palpitating: 51, beating rapidly
gruesome: 51, causing horror
venerable: 51, worthy of honor
lair: 52, the living place of a wild animal
cleaver: 52, a butchering tool
remnants: 52, remains
cunning: 53, clever
vexed: 53, irritated or annoyed

Summary

The expedition heads for Rivendell, where Elrond and the elves live in the Last Homely House west of the mountains that they must cross. After a difficult search, they arrive. Elrond identifies the blades taken from the trolls as having been made for the goblin wars, and names them. He not only reads the plain runes on the map, but discovers runes that can only be read by moonlight. They reveal a mysterious clue to finding the keyhole of the door into Lonely Mountain where the dwarves' treasure now lies.

Writer's Forum

In a compare and contrast essay, you show the similarities and differences between two people, things, ideas, approaches, etc., and draw some conclusion based on this examination. You choose the categories to compare and contrast based on your purpose, and these categories will change depending on your topic. For example, if you were comparing and contrasting Gandalf and Elrond, you might choose categories such as "role in story," "interactions with others," "knowledge," and "appearance." If, however, you were contrasting the setting in Chapter 1 with the setting in Chapter II, you would use different categories. A Venn diagram or a chart can help you organize the information you will use.

A Venn diagram can help to show visually what two or more subjects have or don't have in common. Here is an example diagramming Gandalf and Elrond:

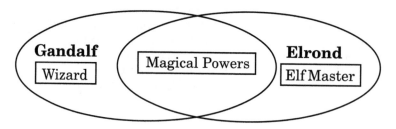

Gandalf — Wizard   Magical Powers   **Elrond** — Elf Master

only Gandalf   common traits   only Elrond

There are two standard ways of organizing a compare and contrast essay. In the **point-by-point method**, you mention each category and all the information about it for both of the things you are considering. For the category "role in story," you might write:

> Gandalf, a wandering wizard, seems to have the role of initiating action and assisting in the quest as a participant. Elrond, the Elvenking, on the other hand, provides the help he can at the moment, but has no long-term commitment to the company.

In the other style of organization, the **block method**, you would first cover every category for one of the things you are considering, and then the other. So you would say everything you had to say about Gandalf (or Elrond) and then everything you had to say about Elrond (or Gandalf).

Source words that can help you express concepts of similarity and difference include the following:

- as well as
- similarly
- differ
- whereas
- however
- likewise
- alike
- while
- but
- on the contrary
- at the same time
- resemble
- conversely
- though
- on the other hand

1. Write an essay comparing and contrasting the trolls and the elves.

Strategy 5

Rhetoric

Rhetoric means either the art of persuasion or the techniques used by writers in their craft. It includes considerations of sentence structure such as **parallelism** (the repetition of grammatical structures), for example:

> "As soon as I clapped eyes on the little fellow bobbing and puffing on the mat, I had my doubts. . . . As soon as I saw your funny faces on the door-step, I had my doubts." pages 17–18

It also includes the techniques called "rhetorical figures" or "figures of speech." The rhetorical figures include the following:

- **Simile:** a comparison using words such as *like*, *as*, or *as if*
  > "It had a perfectly round door like a porthole. . ." page 1

- **Metaphor:** a comparison in which two things which are in fact different are equated
  > "On silver necklaces they strung/The flowering stars . . ." page 14 (either flowering stars is a metaphor for jewels, or if it is taken literally, the dwarves had extraordinary powers)

- **Ellipsis:** leaving out part of a grammatical structure when the structure is repeated several times, on the assumption that it will be understood
  > "It was a hard path and a dangerous path, a crooked way and a lonely [way] and a long [way]. page 55

- **Hyperbole:** exaggeration or overstatement used for emphasis
  > "Excitable little fellow . . . Gets funny queer fits, but he is . . . as fierce as a dragon in a pinch." page 17

- **Personification:** attributing human characteristics to non-human (often inanimate) things
  > ". . . they saw that the great mountains had marched down very near to them . . ." page 45

- **Metonymy:** one thing is used as a substitute for another with which it is closely associated
  > "You've et a village and a half between yer . . ." page 35 (*village* is substituted for *villagers*)

- **Pun:** use of multiple meanings of words that are homophones or homographs to make a word play
  > "And please don't cook me, kind sirs! I am a good cook myself, and cook better than I cook, if you see what I mean." page 37

- **Onomatopoeia:** the use of words that echo the meaning they represent
  > "ding-dong-a-ling-dang" page 9

Other rhetorical devices include **idioms**, expressions the meaning of which can't be figured out from the words themselves.

1. Find three similes and write them with their page numbers.

2. Write the meaning of the following idioms: time out of mind, page 2; going off into the Blue, page 5; put your foot in it, page 18; a nice pickle they were all in, page 39; caught their eyes, page 42; in the nick of time, page 43; we shall be done for, page 46.

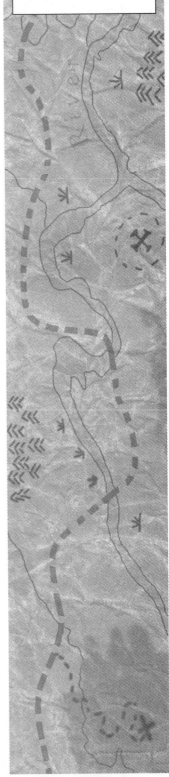

Strategy 6

Maps

Directions: Read the explanation, then answer the questions.

A **map** is a flat representation of part or all of the real world or an imaginary world. A number of journey stories have maps to help the reader become acquainted with the geography of the world of the story. Mysteries may also have maps if an understanding of the layout of a house or larger area is essential to grasping the story. Some of the elements found on most maps and included on the maps in *The Hobbit* include:

- **Title:** maps can be labeled with a title that identifies the location.
- **Compass Rose:** A compass rose identifies the cardinal directions (north, south, east, and west) with respect to the layout of the map. Modern maps have north at the top.
- **Blow Up:** A small section of a map that is drawn larger to show more detail. Sometimes it is inset into the larger map.
- **Symbols:** Most maps have a legend that identifies the symbols. Tolkien uses symbols that he expects us to recognize without aid.
- **Distance and Size:** Tolkien did not provide a bar scale to indicate how the distance on the map relates to the distance in Middle-earth. We can still assume that for A, B, and C on the map, if C is twice as far from A as B is from A, that this relationship mirrors the relationship in the world of Middle-earth.
- **Labels:** Tolkien includes labels for important places, as well as runes that give additional information about the contents of the maps (see pages 21–22).

1. Compare the compass roses on the two maps. Explain how they relate.

2. Which map shows a larger area and which is a blow-up? How can you tell?

3. Use the map to identify a route the company might take. Looking at the symbols on the map, what adventures would you expect they might have if they travel the route you choose?

4. Look at the table of contents to review the chapter titles. What does the information there suggest about the route they might take? Can you match any chapter titles with places on the map?

Strategy 7

Runes is the name of several alphabets used by Germanic peoples from the third to the thirteenth centuries. In the maps for *The Hobbit*, Tolkien treated them like a substitution cipher for English; that is, in most cases each rune represents one English letter. Exceptions: There are one-symbol runes for *ea*, *ee*, *eo*, *ng*, *oo*, *st*, and *th*, as well as a two-symbol rune for q. Also *i* and *j* are represented by the same rune, as are *u* and *v*. Dots mark spaces between words.

Decipher the two rune inscriptions on Thror's Map. The last two letters of the first inscription are Thror's and Thrain's initials. Use this transcription scheme as a guide. Also answer the two questions which follow.

RUNES	ᚠᛒᛀᛞᛖᛘᚷᚺᛁ ᛀᛋᛏᚿᛕᛋᛟᛞᚱ	**RUNES**
	A B C D E F G H I/J K L M N O P Q R	
	ᛋᛏᛌ ᛈᛃᚩᚦᚻᛝᛚ ᚿᛉᛇᛤᛦᛩᛨᛢ	
	S T U/V W X Y Z EA EE EO NG OO ST TH	

Rune Inscription 1: Thror's Map

ᚠᛁᛚᛖ·ᚠᛟᛏ·ᚺᛁᚷᚺ·ᚦᛖ·ᛞᛟᛞᚱ·ᚠᛁᛞ·

_____

Translation

ᚦᛟᛋ·ᛗᚫᚫᚫ·ᚹᚫᛚᚴ·ᚠᛖᛒᚱᛖᚫᛋᛏ: ·ᚦ·ᚦ·

_____

Translation

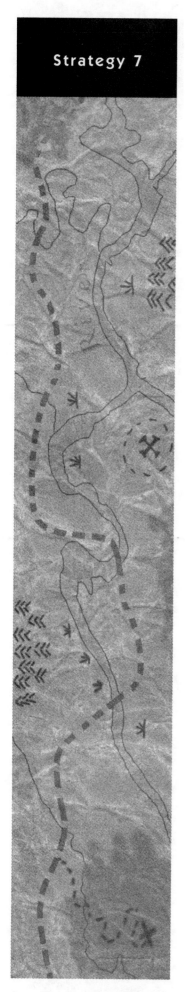

Rune Inscription 2: Thror's Map

ᛋᛏᚨᛜ·ᛒᚨᚦᛖᚷᛘᛖᚨ·ᛋᛏᛟᛖᚺᚹᛖᛜ·

_____
<small>Translation</small>

ᚦᛖ·ᚦᚱᛟᚢᛋ·ᚺᛏᛖᚺᛋ·ᚠᛏᚨᚦᛖ·ᛋᛖᛏᛏᛁᛉ·

_____
<small>Translation</small>

ᛋᛟᛜᚹᛁᚦᛖ·ᚺᛋᛏ·ᛏᛁᚷᚺᛏ·ᛖᚠ·ᛞᚢᚱᛁᛋᛋ·

_____
<small>Translation</small>

ᛞᛖᚨ·ᚹᛁᛚᛚ·ᛋᚺᛁᛟᛖ·ᚢᚴᛟᛜ·ᚦᛖ·

_____
<small>Translation</small>

ᚺᛖᚨᚺᚠᛖᛖ

_____
<small>Translation</small>

1. ᚹᚨᚨ·ᛁᛋ·ᚦᛖ·ᛋᛁᛜᛖ·ᚠᛁ·ᚦᛖ·ᛞᛟᚱ·
   ᛁᛜᚴᛖᚱᛏᚨᛁᛏ?

2. ᚹᚺᚠᛏ·ᚹᛖᛚᛞ·ᚨᚱᛁ·ᛟᛞᛜ·ᛏᚠ·
   ᚺᛏᚨᚠ·ᛏᚠ·ᛁᛞᛖᛜᛏᛁᚠᚨ·ᛞᚢᚱᛁᛋᛋ·
   ᛞᛖᚨ?

Chapter 4   "Over Hill and Under Hill"

Journal and Discussion Topics

1. What mistake do the dwarves make about Durin's Day? What does this tell you about them?
2. What hints does the narrator give that the cave will not be the safe shelter they hope for?
3. How does Bilbo help the company this time?
4. Characterize the goblins.
5. How does Thorin deal with the Great Goblin?
6. Draw a picture based on an image you have in your mind from reading this chapter.
7. What words does Tolkien use that appeal to your sense of hearing in this chapter? Which ones would you say are onomatopoetic?
8. Give an example of parallelism in this chapter.
9. If you had been in the company, what might you have done to try to save yourself and your party from the goblins?

Vocabulary

deceptions: 55, tricks
infested: 55, filled with [something bad]
uncanny: 55, supernatural, eerie
thriven: 56, past tense of thrive, grown well
astray: 56, away from what is desired
drenched: 57, soaked
guffawing: 57, laughing in loud bursts
nooks: 58, sheltered places
champing: 59, chewing
yammer: 61, cries of distress or whining
bleat: 61, complain with sound like a sheep

shirk: 61, avoid work or responsibility
quaff: 61, to drink deeply
rummaged: 61, made a thorough search
alliances: 62, political partnerships
grudge: 62, deep feeling of hatred
warrant: 63, declare with certainty
jibbering: 64, chattering unintelligibly
jabbering: 64, talking quickly & unclearly
skriking: 64, giving a shrill, harsh cry
hordes: 66, crowds or throngs
realm: 67, kingdom

Summary

The company begins their ascent of the Misty Mountains, which they must pass to get to Wilderland beyond. They take shelter from a thunderstorm in a cave that they have not thoroughly explored, and settle down to rest. As they sleep, a crack opens at the back of the cave. Through the crack, goblins appear and steal the baggage and ponies. They take everyone captive except Gandalf, who vanishes in a flash of light when a cry from Bilbo alerts him to the danger. The party is herded underground to an audience with the Great Goblin. Although Thorin presents the group as traveling to a family reunion, their swords reveal them as enemies of goblins. As the goblins attack them, Gandalf reappears and leads them down a passage. They pause once in the their flight to fight and rout one group of goblins, and then hurry on. But more goblins appear and launch a surprise attack during which Bilbo falls from Dori's back where he was riding, hits his head, and blacks out.

Strategy 8

Point of View

Directions:
Read the expla-
nation, then
answer the ques-
tions.

A story is always told by someone. This person is called the narrator. The narrator may be someone who participates in the action of the story, or someone outside the action of the story. The narrator may have a limited range of knowledge, or may know everything there is to know about the story. The narrator may be reliable or unreliable. All of these factors go into what is called the story's **point of view.**

Stories can be told in the **first-person point of view.** In this case, the narrator is usually someone who was present or involved in the action of the story, and this person tells the story using the pronoun *I* to indicate personal involvement.

Stories can also be told in the **second-person point of view,** which is distinguished by the fact that the narrator speaks to the reader as *you,* and addresses the reader directly, as if they were speaking together.

The **third-person point of view** is the point of view of a narrator who is separate from the action and tells it from a greater distance than a first-person narrator would.

A narrator can be **omniscient,** knowing all the action of the story even including what is going on in all the characters' minds and knowing what will happen before it happens, or **limited** to knowledge of only the perspective of one character.

Stories can have mixed points of view. In *The Hobbit,* the narrator sometimes addresses the reader directly and sometimes gives third-person omniscient narration.

It is an essential point that the reader cannot assume that the narrator of a story is the author. Usually the narrator of a work of fiction is a persona created by the author for the purpose of conveying the story.

1. Find three passages that you have read so far that have the second-person point of view. Describe what you think is the narrator's tone toward the reader.

2. Find a passage that shows the narrator's access to Bilbo's inner thoughts and feelings.

3. Find a passage that shows the narrator's access to Gollum's inner thoughts and feelings.

4. What seems to be the narrator's relationship to the events of the story?

Strategy 9   Fantasy

Directions:
Read the explanation, then answer the questions.

Fantasy is fiction that has some elements in common with fairy tales, some elements in common with epic, and other elements in common with science fiction.

Fantasy and science fiction are genres that incorporate elements that are not real. They may both use magic, imaginary creatures and imaginary settings.

Fantasy and epic can both focus on the adventures or journey of a hero who overcomes great odds, and both can incorporate elements of mythology, including gods and goddesses.

"Fairy-story" is actually the term used by Tolkien for his writing. Tolkien says that fairy stories are not just stories about fairies—little creatures with wings that live in flowers—but stories about the realm of Faërie from which fairies come. Faërie is the land that contains elves, dwarves, trolls, and dragons. But there are other essential characteristics. For example, in Faërie, good and beautiful go together, just as evil and ugliness are allied. Evil may sometimes cloak itself in beauty, but goodness creates beauty; it cannot be repugnant. Much of what is called fantasy today has elements from what Tolkien calls "fairy-stories." Here are some of the elements that *The Hobbit* shares with other fantasy stories:

- dragons
- elves
- golden treasure
- harps
- magic
- swords
- water

- dwarves
- goblins
- good and evil
- invisibility
- ring
- trolls
- wizards

Some of the creatures listed above may have different roles and features in different stories, but have some standard characteristics that never change. **Dwarves** are a short race, separate from men, with long beards. They wear long pointed caps, and work as smiths in underground forges. **Trolls** are usually giants or great ogres who are strong, stupid cannibals. They characteristically guard treasures and their lives are ended by exposure to sunlight. **Wizards, elves,** and **goblins,** however, are different in Tolkien's conception than in many other tales.

1. Write descriptions of the characteristics of wizards and elves based on what you've read so far in *The Hobbit*.

2. Compare and contrast the characterization of trolls or dwarves in this book with those in another story you know.

Vocabulary

Look at each group of words. Tell why it is important in the story.

1. scuttled, flustered, flummoxed _____

    _____

2. guffawing, yammer, bleat, jibbering, jabbering, skriking _____

    _____

3. ere, yore, hoard, wrought, delves _____

    _____

4. gullies, ravines, bogs _____

    _____

5. scabbards, hilts, cleaver _____

    _____

Essay Topics

1. Look back at the predictions you made about the book in response to Strategy 1. Write a reflection on those predictions based on what you know now. Make new predictions for the rest of the book.

2. Certain types of imaginary creatures—dwarves, elves, trolls (or ogres), goblins— figure largely in this story. Think of another story you know that features one of these kinds of creatures. Compare and contrast the role of the creatures in that story with their role in *The Hobbit*.

3. Pick a story that you think has a plot like *The Hobbit* so far. Explain the similarities you find.

4. What's your favorite moment in the story so far? Explain why.

5. Which character is your favorite? Tell why.

6. Rewrite a scene from the story, altering it by changing the point of view to one of the characters in the scene.

7. Retell a part of the story using at least five rhetorical figures.

Chapter 5   "Riddles in the Dark"

Journal and Discussion Topics

1. How did Gollum get his name? What does he call himself and why?
2. In your opinion, who wins the riddle contest? Explain.
3. What special properties does Bilbo discover in the dagger and ring? How does he find out?
4. Gollum concludes that Bilbo's first statement to him was a lie. Why?
5. How does Bilbo treat Gollum? How does Gollum treat Bilbo? What motivates them?
6. What aspect of Gollum's character was the most striking to you? Why?

Vocabulary

glimmer: 70, shine faintly
subterranean: 70, underground
unbeknown: 71, not known
slinked: 71, moved secretly
chestnut: 74, stale through repeating
wretch: 75, deserving to be despised
scrumptiously: 76, deliciously
sacred: 79, not to be violated lightly
antiquity: 79, oldness
oddments: 80, leftovers, odds and ends
scrabbling: 81, groping frantically
shambling: 85, shuffling awkwardly

durstn't: 85, dare not
betterment: 86, improvement
resolve: 86, sense of sureness
filtering: 87, shining, but not fully
smote: 88, past tense of smite; struck
hither: 88, to this place
thither: 88, to that place
outcry: 88, noise, clamor
to-do: 88, stir, commotion
ventured: 88, dared, risked
ajar: 89, slightly open
hallooing: 89, crying out loudly

Summary

When Bilbo regains consciousness, he is in the dark. Groping around, he finds a ring on the floor of the tunnel, and carelessly puts it in his pocket. Not knowing how to escape from the goblins' realm, he decides to just go forward. By the glimmer of light that radiates from his dagger, he begins to move along the passage. An underwater lake stops his progress. As he pauses to reflect on what he should do next, Gollum, a hobbit who has lived underground in the goblins' realm for many years, approaches Bilbo, coming across the lake in his little boat. He intends to catch Bilbo and eat him, but hesitates when he sees Bilbo's dagger. Bilbo naively tells Gollum his name and exactly what his situation is. Gollum suggests that they tell riddles, but quickly turns the game into a competition. If Gollum wins, he will eat Bilbo. If Bilbo wins, Gollum will show him the way out of the goblins' realm. Bilbo wins the competition with his last question: "What have I got in my pocket?" Gollum cannot guess, but he soon surmises that Bilbo has found Gollum's magic ring of invisibility, which he had lost only a few hours earlier. Gollum begins to follow Bilbo, and Bilbo—who guesses from Gollum's whisperings that the ring he has found is what Gollum wants—slips it onto his own finger. As Bilbo turns, he sees Gollum coming up behind him, and as he runs away in terror he falls and is astonished when Gollum rushes past him without seeing him. Bilbo realizes that the ring is magical and makes its wearer invisible. Meanwhile, Gollum—thinking that Bilbo knows the power of the ring and has lied about not knowing his way out—heads for the back door, believing that he is following Bilbo. Bilbo, in reality, follows Gollum, who leads him right to the exit, and then sits, blocking the path. Bilbo, in desperation, leaps over Gollum's head, uses the invisibility provided by the ring to evade the goblin guards, and escapes through the back door into daylight. Because the sun is still shining, the goblins quickly give up the search and return to the dark.

Strategy 10 Plot Conflict

Directions: Read the explanation, then answer the questions.

Conflict is the core of a story's plot. Conflict is what makes us wonder if the protagonist will attain his or her goal. Conflict is what adds suspense and excitement to stories. Usually there is one overarching conflict that takes up much of the book. But each chapter or scene in the book usually also has conflict on a smaller scale.

The struggles that a protagonist undergoes in a story can be either **internal** or **external**. In an **internal** conflict, the protagonist undergoes an interior struggle. He or she might have conflicting desires, values, personality traits, and/or motives. People often have internal conflict as they grow and develop from one stage in their lives to the next. An internal conflict takes place in the character's mind and heart.

In an **external** conflict, the protagonist struggles with something or someone outside of himself or herself. The conflict may be with another individual, with a task or problem, with society, with nature, with an idea, or with a force, such as good or evil.

1. What is the overarching conflict in this story? Cite evidence to support your conclusion.

2. Skim Chapters 1–5 to find the conflicts and enter them on the chart. Then as you continue reading, make entries for each new chapter.

CHAPTER	CONFLICT
1	
2	
3	
4	
5	
6	
7	
8	
9	
10	
11	
12	
13	
14	
15	
16	
17	
18	
19	

Chapter 6

"Out of the Frying-Pan and into the Fire"

Journal and Discussion Topics

1. How does Bilbo react to the loss of the company? How does the company react to the loss of Bilbo? What conclusions can you draw?
2. Compare and contrast Bilbo's story of what happened to him with what the narrator said happened to him. How do you account for the differences? What would you have done if you were Bilbo?
3. How has Bilbo changed since Chapter 1?
4. Riddle competitions have been used since primitive times to decide the fate of someone or something. How is this tradition reflected in the company's reaction to Bilbo's story?
5. What functions does the setting serve in this chapter?
6. One of the techniques Tolkien uses to support the conceit that the narrator is relating true history is to make connections between the origins of real-world language and the imaginary world of the story. In Chapter 1 (page 17), he has the narrator explain the origins of the game of golf. How does he use this technique in Chapter 6?

Vocabulary

dells: 91, small, hidden valleys
helter-skelter: 92, in confusion
benighted: 94, overtaken by night
bewitchments: 94, spells
turf: 96, grass
thyme: 96, a garden herb in the mint family
sage: 96, herb used for food and healing
marjoram: 96, herb in the mint family
onslaught: 97, a fierce attack
bracken: 97, large coarse ferns
fronds: 97, large leaves of ferns

glade: 98, open area surrounded by woods
porter: 99, someone who carries burdens
clambered: 100, climbed awkwardly
clamour/clamor: 100, a noisy shouting
pinnacle: 103, the highest point
afoot: 104, under way
reek: 105, smoke
talons: 106, claws of a bird of prey
tumult: 107, the uproar made by a crowd
giddy: 107, dizzy
eyrie: 107, a bird's nest on a mountaintop

Summary

Bilbo realizes that he has crossed through the mountains to the eastern side, but he has no idea where his companions are. He has just decided that it is his duty to return to the goblin realm to find and rescue them if possible, when he hears voices. Following the sound, he comes upon the dwarves arguing with Gandalf, who insists that it is their duty to return to the goblins' realm to find and, if possible, rescue Bilbo. Bilbo uses the ring to walk into their midst unseen and surprise them. This, as well as his tale of escape, impresses them and raises him in their estimation, especially as he chooses not to reveal to them the existence of the ring. Gandalf explains how Bilbo disappeared and reappeared, and warns the party that they must hurry away for as soon as it is dark, the goblins will be tracking them. They scramble and tumble down the mountain into a pine forest, where suddenly they hear the howl of wolves. Climbing into the trees keeps them safe at first, but Gandalf, listening in on the wolves' (or wargs') conversation, realizes that the wolves are in league with the goblins. In this desperate situation, he begins lighting pine cones with a magic fire and heaving them at the wolves. But the goblins soon arrive and use the burning cones to set fires around the trees where the company is perched. Gandalf is about to leap down from the trees and sacrifice himself in an attempt to save the others, when eagles, led by their lord, swoop down and snatch all of the company away to safety, carrying them to the eyrie, where they feed them and let them rest.

Strategy 11

Directions: Read the explanation, then answer the questions.

Writers do not always tell plot events in chronological order. They may hint at events before their place in the sequence. This is called **foreshadowing,** and it lets readers know beforehand something about what is going to happen later. This technique helps create suspense and keeps the reader involved in the unfolding plot.

Foreshadowing may come from a character, from the setting, or from the narrator. For example, Gandalf says of Bilbo, "If I say he is a Burglar, a Burglar he is, or will be when the time comes" (page 19). If you think that Gandalf is reliable, you may conclude that Bilbo is going to undergo a transformation during the story that allows him to act in the role of a burglar before the end.

The change of setting on page 31 is another example of foreshadowing. It is described like this: "Not far ahead were dreary hills, rising higher and higher, dark with trees. On some of them were old castles with an evil look, as if they had been built by wicked people." This setting suggests that the company is moving into dangerous territory.

When, after Bilbo has commented, "I wish I was at home in my nice hole by the fire, with the kettle just beginning to sing!", the narrator comments, "It was not the last time that he wished that!", it suggests that trials and tribulations are going to be a major part of the plot.

Writers may also go back to material that happened prior to the beginning of the story or earlier in the plot sequence. This is called **flashback.** Flashbacks give the reader necessary background material for understanding the story. Flashbacks may come from the narrator or the characters. When Thorin, for example, begins his tale of the treasure on page 22, "Long ago in my grandfather Thror's time . . . ," this is a flashback. When the narrator fills in details about Gollum and his relationship with the ring on page 81, "Gollum used to wear it at first, till it tired him . . . " this, too, is flashback. Flashback is part of the exposition in a novel.

1. Find another example of a flashback. What essential information does it contain?

2. Find 3 different examples of foreshadowing. Are they from characters, the setting, or the narrator? What conclusions did you draw from them while you were reading?

Chapter 7   "Queer Lodgings"

Journal and Discussion Topics

1. Explain Gandalf's trick. Why does he choose this way of bringing the company to Beorn's house?
2. How does Beorn's attitude towards the company change over time?
3. Compare and contrast Beorn and Elrond.
4. How does Beorn help the company?
5. What trust does Gandalf lay on Bilbo? Do you think Bilbo can fulfill it? Why or why not?

Vocabulary

cropping: 112, appearing unexpectedly
ford: 112, shallow place to cross a river
appalling: 114, causing horror or dismay
furrier: 114, animal trapper and fur trader
conies: 114, rabbits; term used by poachers
tippet: 115, fur cape
muff: 115, fur handwarmer
droning: 116, deep humming, buzzing sound
drones: 116, male bees
thatched: 117, roofed with straw
lopped: 117, taken off as no longer needed
tunic: 117, knee-length, sleeveless garment
unimpeachable: 118, blameless; perfect
reputation: 118, judgment about character
veranda: 118, roofed porch
westering: 119, moving toward the west
brackets: 124, fixtures to hold torches

trestles: 124, frames used as supports
perils: 125, dangers
mould/mold: 126, in Brit. dialect, ground
waistcoat: 130, vest
vengeance: 130, punishment in revenge
lade: 131, to put a load on
drowsiness: 132, readiness for sleep
scour: 133, search thoroughly
glowered: 134, etymology unclear: glowed; or scowled, understood figuratively
browsing: 134, eating twigs and leaves
harts: 134, male red deer; stags
gnarled 134, twisted with swellings
wearisomely: 136, exhaustingly
trudging 136, marching steadily
quest: 137, adventurous journey with a goal
temptation: 137, a strong desire

Summary

As soon as the eagles have carried their guests down from the eyrie to a resting place on the plain, Gandalf announces that he has other business to attend to and reminding the party that this is not his adventure, expresses his intention to part company from them after helping them to find food, baggage, and ponies. The dwarves offer him treasure, and Bilbo weeps, but Gandalf is adamant. Gandalf then leads them to Beorn's home, where he gains a warm welcome for them by playing a trick on the usually inhospitable berserker. He goes to Beorn's home accompanied only by Bilbo, leaving orders for the dwarves to come by twos at intervals. Then he begins a story of their adventures which fascinates Beorn so much that he accepts the fifteen visitors more or less graciously. Waited on by Beorn's talking animals, they spend a pleasant evening, while Beorn, transforming himself into a bear, roams the land, checking on the veracity of Gandalf's tale. Finding it true, he engages to help them by providing ponies and food, and advises them to take the elf path farther north. Beorn secretly accompanies their ride north to guard and guide the company, as well as to make sure they release his ponies before they enter Mirkwood. He gives the company three pieces of advice: it is hard to find water in Mirkwood and there is probably nothing wholesome there to eat or drink; they should not touch or drink the water in the black stream; they should not go off the path. As they reach Mirkwood, Gandalf leaves, commending the dwarves to Bilbo's care, saying, "You have got to look after all these dwarves for me."

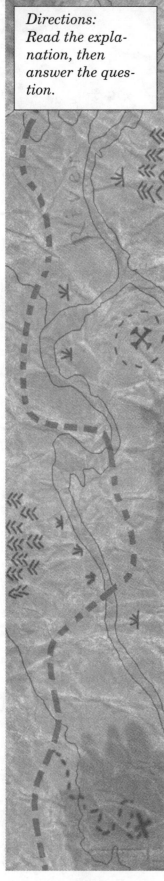

Strategy 12   Setting and Mood

Directions: Read the explanation, then answer the question.

Setting, meaning the changing scenery that serves as the backdrop for each scene or chapter in a book, is connected to the feeling or **mood** that scene or chapter evokes. Think about the settings that have occurred in the book thus far. Chapter 1 begins with the comfortable, homey setting of Bilbo's house. In Chapter 2, the setting becomes unwelcoming, and the company encounters the trolls. In Chapter 3, the company arrives at Rivendell, the delightful home of the elves. In Chapter 4, the company is captured by the goblins and taken underground. Are you beginning to see a pattern of friendly, welcoming settings alternated with threatening settings in which a foe is waiting?

1. As you read each chapter, record the settings that are used and the plot development that takes place. Then record the mood of each setting. Afterwards, write about the patterns you see.

CHAPTER	SETTING – PLOT ACTION – MOOD
1	
2	
3	
4	
5	
6	
7	
8	
9	
10	
11	
12	
13	
14	
15	
16	
17	
18	
19	

Writer's Forum

Diary Entry

In a diary entry, you record the important events of the day from your own point of view. Diaries may also link the present to the past or include hopes, dreams, or plans for the future.

Some part of a diary might be rather objective, while others might be very personal and subjective. Diary writing is often informal—because people usually write diaries for themselves, they don't follow all the rules of grammar, punctuation, and usage. People may use words with private meanings, abbreviations, etc.

Diaries are not necessarily all your own words. Some people choose to add quotations of others' words that they find helpful, interesting, or meaningful. Some people have a combination diary and scrapbook. Others draw in their diaries. Since a diary is personal, it can take many forms.

1. Choose a character from this book. Write four diary entries for that character. You may wish to write one for each of several chapters, or you can find your own way of deciding what to write about. Feel free to embellish and elaborate, while staying "in character."

Chapter 8

"Flies and Spiders"

Journal and Discussion Topics

1. Explain how the setting is important to the plot of this chapter.
2. What dangers does the company encounter in Mirkwood?
3. What strategies does Bilbo use to outwit the spiders?
4. What change occurs in Bilbo with the killing of the first spider?
5. What secret does Bilbo share with the dwarves? Why?

Vocabulary

lichen: 139, plant matter on flat surfaces
inquisitive: 139, very curious
bulbous: 140, round like a bulb
taut: 143, drawn tight
painter: 143, a line used for tying a boat
falter: 144, become unsteady
straggle: 145, wander from a direct route
funguses: 146, plants like mushrooms
disquieting: 146, removing peace and calm
accursed: 147, deserving to be cursed
grimed: 147, covered with dirt
tuppence: 148, British coin worth 2 pennies
parchingly: 149, to the point of scorching
blundering: 151, moving in a confused way
dratted: 152, a mild oath
twined: 153, woven

glinted: 153, gleamed, shone
abominable: 154, causing disgust
lamented: 155, complained; said sorrowfully
stealthily: 156, secretly
cosily/cozily: 157, snugly; in a cozy way
stoop: 157, bend down
snares: 158, noose traps for birds and game
infuriate: 158, to make furious
froth: 160, foamy saliva that drips
goggling: 162, staring with eyes bulging
hacking: 164, chopping
wary: 166, cautious and watchful
gloaming: 167, twilight
tilling: 168, plowing, sowing, raising crops
thongs: 168, strips of leather

Summary

The company proceeds through Mirkwood and comes to the black stream. They manage to snare a boat and all cross safely until it is Bombur's turn. He falls into the river, and when they pull him out, he is fast asleep and cannot be wakened. They are forced to carry him. They begin to despair of ever getting out of the forest. As they finish the last of their food and start to run out of water, they become desperate. While they are in this susceptible state, Bombur awakens and begins to recount dreams of a woodland king with a crown of leaves who is holding a feast with incredible food. The company decides that their hunger takes precedence over the warning not to leave the path. When they see lights in the woods, they try three times to approach the feast, and each time the lights go out, the elves flee, and the company has an increasingly difficult time finding each other again. The last time, Bilbo is separated from all the rest. He falls asleep and awakens to find his legs wrapped in cobweb. He draws his dagger, slashes himself free, and kills the spider who is wrapping him. This act has a powerful effect on Bilbo's self-image, and at this moment he names his dagger, dubbing it "Sting." Bilbo puts on the ring and sets out to look for his friends who have all been captured by the spiders, wrapped in cobwebs, and hung from a branch. He first attacks the spiders with stones, then uses a taunting song to draw them away from their prey, doubles back while the spiders are out of sight, and cuts the dwarves down. But the spiders return, so Bilbo tells the dwarves about the ring, to help them understand what he's doing, and again leads the spiders away so the dwarves can escape. The dwarves' respect for Bilbo increases immeasurably. But soon they realize that Thorin is missing. Without their knowledge, the Elvening has captured Thorin and imprisoned him.

Strategy 13

Character

Directions: Read the explanation, then answer the questions.

We often speak of **Character** traits as being absolutes—that is, characters either have them or not. So we might describe a character as greedy and obnoxious. This is useful for a start. But even a character that we recognize as greedy and obnoxious in general can be more or less greedy and more or less obnoxious, depending on the situation. Considering the variations in character traits can be the first step in taking a more realistic view of the complex thing we call character. We can consider character traits as existing on a continuum, a scale with opposite traits at the ends and a whole range of possible points in between. For example:

hospitable————————————————inhospitable

Think about Bilbo: he's generally a hospitable, friendly character. Now think about Chapter 1. Bilbo's initial greeting to Gandalf (page 4) is hospitable and welcoming. But during the course of the chapter, his hospitality and welcome are severely tested, and at times he is downright rude. You can see that to say that Bilbo is or isn't hospitable would not come near to telling the whole story.

1. For each continuum, write a paragraph telling how the indicated character(s) move(s) along it during the course of the book.

generosity———selfishness
(Bilbo, dwarves, the Master)

uncertainty————self-confidence
(Bilbo)

honesty———deception
(Gollum, Bilbo, dwarves,
Thorin)

leadership—abrogation of responsibility
(Bilbo, Gandalf, Thorin, the Master,
Bard)

2. Choose a single character and write a full-page description of his character traits. Explain how his behavior varies along each continuum that you identify.

Chapter 9 "Barrels Out of Bond"

Journal and Discussion Topics

1. What leads the Elvenking to imprison the dwarves?
2. Describe Bilbo's initial reaction to the company's imprisonment. How does his reaction change?
3. How do luck and planning combine to make the escape possible?
4. This is the second time Bilbo has freed the dwarves. Compare and contrast the two rescues.
5. Compare and contrast the elves' song on pages 182-183 with the goblins' song on pages 60–61. Consider the purpose, audience, points of reference, and the sound of the poetry.

Vocabulary

hewn: 171, cut to shape
carven: 171, same as carved
surly: 172, irritable and arrogant
remotest: 172, most distant
nimble: 173, quick in motion
dreariest: 173, most discouraging
ransom: 174, obtain release of a prisoner by exchange of goods for freedom
plight: 174, difficult situation
portcullis: 175, a grate to block a passage
lurking: 175, lying in wait in a hidden place
throve: 176, p.t. of thrive; prospered
flagons: 177, large containers for wine
potent: 177, strong; powerful
heady: 177, able to make drunk
vintage: 177, a season's yield of wine

justified: 178, shown to be reasonable
downcast: 178, depressed
adjoining: 179, attached side-by-side
kennel: 180, shelter for a dog
slowcoach: 180, slow or lazy person
draught: 181, Brit. for draft, a dose of liquid
turnkey: 181, person in charge of the keys to a prison
jostling: 181, bumping
mere: 183, a lake
kine: 183, archaic plural of cow
eddying: 184, going in circles
shingly: 185, full of gravel as a beach
suppressed: 186, stopped
fretted: 186, rubbed together

Summary

The next day, the wood-elves find the company and capture all the dwarves. Bilbo, slipping on his ring, escapes notice and is able to follow along. The Elvenking questions them, but resenting their impolite manner, imprisons them. Bilbo, realizing that he is the only one who can obtain their release, locates the cells of all the dwarves, and they put their trust in him. The narrator suggests that part of Gandalf's reason for leaving the group was to effect this change. For a while, Bilbo is stumped for a rescue plan. One day he spots the trapdoors through which barrels for wine and foodstuffs are dropped into the stream to be rafted back to Lake-town, the source of the elves' provisions. Fortuitously, Bilbo overhears a conversation that reveals that the chief guard is going to spend the evening drinking with the king's butler while the king holds a feast. Bilbo takes advantage of the chief guard's intoxicated sleep to steal his keys and release the dwarves. Bilbo explains his plan, and although the dwarves do not like it, they allow Bilbo to pack them into barrels. He completes this task only moments before elves arrive to begin their work of dropping the barrels into the stream. Although some of the casks feel heavy, making the elves suspect that they've got the wrong batch, they are all rolled into the stream. Bilbo suddenly realizes that he has not planned his own escape. He grabs onto the last barrel and lands on it in the icy water. At the end of the Forest River, the barrels are roped together into a raft and sent on their journey to the lake, but the narrator indicates that the dwarves may or may not have survived the journey.

Strategy 14   Irony

*Directions:
Read the explanation, then answer the question.*

Irony comes from a Greek word meaning "someone who hides under a false appearance." When irony is used, things appear different, even the opposite, of what they really are: unexpected events happen, what people say is not what they mean. Authors use irony to create interest, surprise, or an understanding with their readers that the characters do not share. There are three types of irony.

Verbal irony is irony in the use of language. Verbal irony means that what is said is different from what is meant. Irony can be conveyed through understatement. When Thorin says to the Great Goblin, "nothing was further from our thoughts than inconveniencing goblins in any way whatever" (page 63), this is an understatement that adds force to the idea he is expressing.

Irony can also be communicated by saying the opposite of what is meant. When the narrator says (page 159) after Bilbo sings his song to the spiders, "They were frightfully angry. Quite apart from the stones no spider has ever liked being called Attercop, and Tomnoddy of course is insulting to anybody," it is an example of verbal irony. You probably wouldn't care at all if someone called you "Tomnoddy," but the narrator acts as if it is a great insult, easily recognized by all, showing us how stupid the spiders are— their whole plot to kill and eat the company, which is practically guaranteed to succeed, is ruined because of one silly word.

In **dramatic irony**, there is knowledge that the narrator makes available to the reader, but the characters are unaware of it. When the narrator tells us on page 68 (when Bilbo finds the ring) that "It was a turning point in his career, but he did not know it," this is an example of dramatic irony. We know and the narrator knows, but Bilbo doesn't.

Situational irony can occur either from the point of view of a character or the reader. It describes a situation when something that is expected with a great deal of certainty doesn't happen (this can be from either point of view) or when something that is intended fails to materialize (this is only possible from a character's point of view, except in Choose-Your-Own Adventures or other books in which the reader participates by making a choice).

When Bilbo tries to pick William's pocket (page 36), he does it intending to impress the dwarves with his skill at burglary. But his action has the opposite effect. As Bombur says (page 42), "Silly time to go practising pinching and pocket-picking."

1. Keep a record of other examples of irony in this story as you review chapters already read and continue to read.

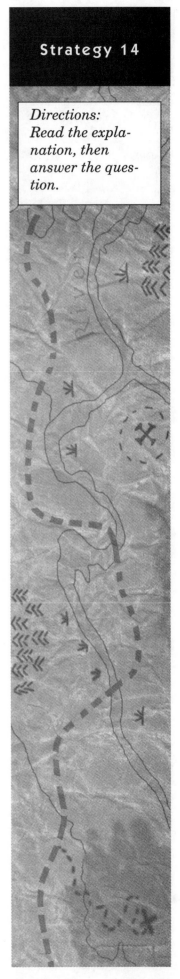

Writer's Forum News Article

A news article gives an objective report of an event that is important to the people who read that particular paper. While the event can be local, national, or international, it must have some impact on or hold some interest for the readership.

The headline of a news article both catches the reader's attention and declares the main topic of the article. Sports or feature articles may have a cryptic headline or one that includes wordplay, to get the reader interested, but news headlines are usually straightforward.

The first paragraph of a news article gives the reader a quick summary of the important details, usually by telling the 5 W's (Who, What, Where, When, and Why) and How. Subsequent paragraphs give additional details that fill out the story.

News stories often include material gathered from interviews. This material may be stated indirectly or directly as quotations. If direct quotations are used, proper capitalization and punctuation should accompany it. Use care to make sure that you write the person's exact words. If you're not sure, ask.

1. Write a news story relating the escape of the company from the wood-elves. You may make up supporting information to add details to the story. You may also decide when the story was released. The story should include an interview with at least one individual to whom the escape was important.

   You may decide the readership of your paper. This will shape how you choose to tell the story. Decide the name of the newspaper you are writing for. Give yourself a byline, and make your story look like a news article. You may include an illustration with a caption if you wish.

Test: Chapters 5–9

Vocabulary

Look at each group of words. Tell why it is important in the story.

1. slinked, scrabbling, shambling _____

_____

2. furrier, conies, tippet, muff _____

_____

3. flagons, potent, heady, vintage _____

_____

4. lichen, fungus, gloaming _____

_____

5. giddy, eyrie _____

_____

Essay Topics

1. Explain each of the riddles in the exchange between Bilbo and Gollum.
2. Compare and contrast the trolls' (page 40), goblins' (pages 105-106), and spiders' (page 156) discussions of how to prepare and eat the members of the company.
3. What's your favorite moment in Chapter's 5–9. Explain why.
4. The story Gandalf tells Beorn can be called an add-on story. In an add-on story, an important plot element is the steady increase of characters or action. There are many add-on stories, some like Gandalf's, some differently structured. The nursery rhymes "This Is the House that Jack Built" and "The Farmer in the Dell" are two other examples. Make up a short add-on story.
5. Find words that have to do with light and dark on pages 139-141. List them. Explain the effect they have.
6. What do you think of the name "Sting" for Bilbo's dagger? What would you have named it? Why?
7. Look up the games listed on page 157. Briefly explain what each one is.
8. Find three examples of foreshadowing in the book so far.
9. In what ways have things changed for the company since Gandalf left? Use details from the text to support your ideas.

Chapter 10   "A Warm Welcome"

Jorurnal and Discussion Topics

1. How does luck continue to be a factor in the plot?
2. Describe the release of the dwarves from the barrels.
3. Explain the guards' reaction to the company.
4. Characterize the Master.
5. Explain the townspeople's reaction to the company.
6. In what way is the Elvenking wrong about the dwarves' plans?
7. What do you think is the meaning of the chapter title, "A Warm Welcome"?

Vocabulary

alluding: 189, referring
ominous: 189, suggesting evil
receded: 190, moved back
Wain: 190, a wagon; the Big Dipper
promontory: 190, a high point of rock that projects into a body of water
prosperous: 191, doing well economically
fleets: 191, a group of ships or planes
drought: 191, period of dry weather
moored: 191, tied up with a line or anchor
buffeted: 192, hit repeatedly
famished: 192, suffering from hunger
floundering: 192, moving clumsily

cramped: 192, confined in too small a space
waterlogged: 193, completely soaked
squabbles: 193, noisy, unimportant quarrels
gammers: 193, archaic term for old women
solemnities: 194, formal occasions
quays: 195, landing places parallel to bank
vagabond: 195, one without a home
molesting: 195, disturbing
hinder: 195, stop
enmity: 196, hatred, each for the other
pampered: 197, treated with care
circuitous: 199, winding

Summary

As Bilbo listens to the raftsmen converse, he learns that the elf road comes to a dead end, and that he has brought the dwarves to the next stage of their journey by the only remaining possible route. After landing at Lake-town, Bilbo waits until night, and then unpacks the miserable dwarves. They make their way to the feast being held by the Master of Lake-town, and Thorin announces the return of the king under the mountain. The elves who came with the raft recognize the dwarves and denounce them as vagabonds. The Master is not sure what to think since he values the Elvenking's friendship and does not believe in the old songs which predict the return of the king and renewed prosperity for the land. But the decision is taken out of his hands by the response of the townspeople, who hail the return of the king. The dwarves become pampered guests of the town, and stay for a fortnight. At the end of this time, Thorin announces his intention to leave. The Master gives them ponies and provision, and they set off for Lonely Mountain.

Chapter 11   "On the Doorstep"

Journal and Discussion Topics
1. What is the role of the setting in this chapter?
2. How do various members of the company react to the closed door?
3. Give some examples of advice the dwarves have not taken so far in the book.
4. Find an example of foreshadowing in this chapter. What do you make of it?
5. Describe the relationship of the dwarves and the hobbit in this chapter.
6. What do you make of the thrush?
7. How does the description of what happens when the door opens affect you?

Vocabulary
desolate: 201, deserted; lifeless
escort: 201, group giving protection
spur: 202, ridge protruding from mountain
plodding: 202, slow moving
gloom: 202, depression; low spirits
bleak: 202, open to the wind and lacking life
barren: 202, bare, without growing thing
desolation: 202, ruin
waning: 202, decreasing in size (of the moon); the opposite of waxing
cavernous: 203, having caverns, deep caves
shuddered: 203, shivered
perilous: 204, dangerous

pondering: 204, thinking deeply about
marauding: 204, roaming to raid and steal
bay: 205, earth formation resembling a bay in the sea
mason's: 205, belonging to a stone worker
lintel: 205, board carrying the load over a door
threshold: 205, plank that lies under door
mishap: 205, unfortunate accident
crannies: 206, small slits or holes
brooded: 206, was getting ready to hatch, like a hen sitting on eggs
glummer: 206, gloomier
vapor: 209, matter in the gaseous state

Summary
When the company reaches Lonely Mountain, after passing through the barren Desolation of Smaug, they make camp on the southern spur of Ravenhill. They assume that Smaug is sleeping within the mountain, but do not check. Then they establish a second camp on the side where the secret door must stand. When they finally find the site of the door, they make their third camp, filled at first with excitement. But as the days pass and they continue to be unable to enter, they become morose and disconsolate. Then, in the last week of autumn, as Bilbo sits one day on the "doorstep," he sees both the sun and the moon in the sky at once. At the same moment, he hears a thrush cracking snails by knocking them against a stone. Bilbo calls to the dwarves, who come running. They wait as the sun seems to finish setting with no fulfillment of the runes. But suddenly a single gleam comes across the sky and lights the door. At Bilbo's urging, Thorin uses his key and unlocks the door. The company pushes the door open and looks into the darkness.

old forest
-road

the shire

wilderland

misty
mountains

Chapter 12   "Inside Information"

Journal and Discussion Topics

1. Write characterizations of Bilbo and the dwarves based on this chapter.
2. What motivates Bilbo to steal the cup?
3. What techniques does Tolkien use to characterize Smaug?
4. Explain how Bilbo tries to trick Smaug and how Smaug tries to influence Bilbo. Is either successful? Explain. Include a clarification of Bilbo's riddle-talk.
5. What mistakes does Bilbo make in dealing with Smaug, in your opinion?
6. What effect does the hoard of gold have on the various characters?

Vocabulary

treacherous: 211, likely to betray; faithless
thrumming: 213, steady humming noise
ruddy: 213, reddish
helms: 213, helmets
staggerment: 213, being thrown into doubt
lust: 214, intense longing; craving
dire: 214, horrifying
cowered: 215, shrank away
insignificant: 215, not important
wrath: 217, anger mixed with vengeance
smouldering: 218, burning without flame
inevitable: 218, not able to be avoided
perplexed: 218, puzzled; uncertain
replenish: 219, to build up again
surpassed: 219, exceeded
whiff: 220, slight suggestion; quick puff
flattered: 220, moved by praise
calamities: 220, major misfortunes
creditable: 221, believable
skulking: 222, concealing oneself to do ill
roving: 222, wandering
grievous: 222, serious
cartage: 223, price for carting goods

wily: 223, sly
unassessably: 223, beyond determination
devastating: 224, causing helplessness
gloated: 224, enjoyed with evil pleasure
fortified: 224, made strong
antiquated: 224, old and out of date
impenetrable: 224, not able to be pierced
dazzlingly: 225, overwhelming with brilliance
flawless: 225, perfect
detain: 225, stop
ghastly: 225, horrible
frizzled: 225, burned; scorched
dubious: 227, uncertain
undercuts: 227, boxing blows
stratagems: 227, tricks used in war
frontal: 227, directed at the front
foreboding: 227, feeling that evil is near
lure: 228, attract into danger
forged: 229, heated and shaped by hammer
facets: 229, small plane surfaces on a cut gem
marrow: 229, fig. deepest part of self
smithereens: 230, bits

Summary

Balin comes part way down the tunnel with Bilbo. Then Bilbo journeys alone, slipping on his ring. When he gets near Smaug, he stops. His decision to go on is the bravest thing he ever did. He finds Smaug asleep on a hoard of untold wealth. Bilbo, almost mesmerized, steals a two-handled cup to prove his ability as a burglar, and runs to show the dwarves. Smaug awakens and immediately misses the cup. He flies out of the gate to find the thief. The dwarves, at Bilbo's urging, go inside the door, which Smaug is unable to find. The company stays safe for the moment, but have to face the weak point of their plan—they have never had a strategy for dealing with Smaug. Bilbo offers to go down to Smaug again and see if an idea comes to him. Now Bilbo has become the "real leader" of the adventure. Bilbo converses with Smaug and unwittingly reveals his connection with Lake-town. He then manages to flatter Smaug into showing his belly, where Bilbo spots a large hollow patch—his only vulnerable spot. Bilbo recounts what he has found to the dwarves, irritated when he realizes the thrush is listening. Suddenly, on Bilbo's intuition, the company retreats into the tunnel and closes the door, just before Smaug comes crashing into the mountain in an attempt to destroy them before hurrying down to attack Lake-town.

Strategy 15

Reference, Allusion and Parody

Directions: Read the explanation, then answer the question.

A **reference** is a mention of something outside the work you are currently reading. It could be a reference to a real or imaginary event, person, or place; or another literary work (often in a quotation); an aspect of culture, or a fact. References are often documented.

An **allusion** is an indirect reference—one that you need to recognize as a reference without the author telling you that it is one. After you recognize the allusion, you need to figure out what it means in the context. Sometimes an author will include clues like quotation marks, or introductory words ("as the great philosopher once said...") or use a name ("as we know so well from Homer"). But sometimes, especially if recognizing and understanding it are not essential to the author's point, the author may not signal the allusion. She or he may, instead, rely on readers sharing a common knowledge of literature, history, biography, science, and art that in most cases will help readers figure out meanings. Or, the allusions may be more like private jokes, inserted for those who can get them. Allusions help the reader see the work as part of a greater literary tradition.

Allusions can have different meanings. Many allusions are to references that support or reinforce the meaning in the text. But this is not the only possible purpose of an allusion. **Parody** is a special type of allusion that recalls to mind something in order to make fun of it through imitation coupled with other devices such as exaggeration and contrast.

You may or may not have recognized that the interactions between Bilbo and Smaug are an allusion to the Old English epic poem *Beowulf* from the eight century. This is a poem that is frequently studied in high school or college, and one that Tolkien studied extensively. Read Parts XXXI-XXXIX of *Beowulf*.

Here is the gist of the part of the epic Tolkien parodies: There is a dragon who has stolen treasure from people and has held it in a hoard for 300 years. But while the dragon sleeps, a man in dire need enters, steals a cup, and takes it to his master to make peace with him. The master grants the man's prayer. But when the dragon awakes, he smells the man and notices the theft. The dragon vows to punish the thief, and set the town on fire. The great hero, Beowulf, faces the dragon alone, and eventually kills it, with help from his kinsman Wiglaf but at the cost of his own life. The word *glede*, which Tolkien uses (page 249), comes from *Beowulf* (line 4614).

1. Explain the ways in which Tolkien alludes to the dragon episode in *Beowulf*. How is Tolkien's treatment a parody?

Chapter 13

"Not at Home"

Journal and Discussion Topics

1. How does the chapter title create dramatic irony?
2. Compare and contrast Bilbo's attitude about going down the tunnel and exploring Smaug's hoard with the dwarves' attitude.
3. What effects does the treasure have on the various characters?
4. How does Bilbo react to Thorin's gift?
5. What changes of setting occur in the chapter? How do they affect mood?
6. Describe the company's situation at the end of the chapter.

Vocabulary

dazed: 232, groggy and insensible
devilry: 232, wickedness
stench: 233, a strong bad smell; a stink
confound: 233, an oath with a curse
alight: 234, being on fire
pallid: 235, pale
radiance: 235, a bright, shining glow
mere: 237, being not more than
fleeting: 237, quickly vanishing
rekindled: 237, lit again
clad: 238, dressed
hafted: 238, handled
goblets: 238, drinking cups for wine

adornments: 239, decorations
mouldered: 239, decayed; crumbled
befouled: 239, made foul
furtive: 239, sly
fluttering: 239, becoming brighter and dimmer without pattern
draughts/drafts 239, currents of air
charred: 239, burnt
decaying: 239, rotting
indefinitely: 242, for an unknown (but long) length of time
sustaining: 242, nourishing
perpetually: 243, continually

Summary

There is no light in the tunnel where the company hides, and the air is becoming stale as they wait for some indication about Smaug's movements. Finding the door permanently blocked, they decide in desperation to go down the tunnel. Bilbo leads the group and falls out of the corridor onto the hoard. Looking around through the treasure while the dwarves cower in the corridor, Bilbo discovers the most valuable item of all, the Arkenstone, and enchanted by it, he puts it in his pocket. Bilbo's light goes out, and he calls on the dwarves who, for once, come to his aid. They then take mail and arm themselves and Bilbo. But soon the dwarves are lost in the enchantment of the gold. It is only when Bilbo recalls them, reminding them of their deadly peril should Smaug return, that they break the spell of the treasure and begin their hike to a safer spot. After looking out the Front Gate, they make their way to the old lookout post on the southwest corner. They search for signs of Smaug without finding anything but a great gathering of birds in the south.

Within the image on the left side are the following signs:

old forest road

the shire

wilderland

misty mountains

Writer's Forum   A Scene from a Play

A play differs from fiction in that there is generally no narration. The play script includes action and words to be spoken, but does not have the plot laid out in narration the way a story (fiction) does. The playwright may give scene directions (tell briefly where geographical features, furniture, etc., are located and what they look like), but it is up to the production designer to fill in the missing details. Similarly, the playwright may give brief descriptions of the way the characters speak and move and interact, but it is up to the designer and actors to fill in the missing details. Plays consist mainly of dialogue and monologue—the words that the characters speak to one another, to themselves, and to the audience.

In other ways, a play is very similar to a work of fiction. It has a protagonist and an antagonist, and a plot that includes exposition, conflict, a climax, and a resolution. These elements are just presented differently in drama than in narrative.

Here is a sample of script format based on a passage from *The Hobbit* on pages 241-242. Notice how the narration is incorporated into stage directions or dialogue.

[Thorin laughs and rattles the precious stones in his pockets.]
THORIN. Come, come! Don't call my palace a nasty hole! You wait till it has been cleaned and redecorated.

BILBO. [*Glumly.*] That won't be till Smaug's dead. In the meanwhile where is he? I would give a good breakfast to know. I hope he is not up on the Mountain looking down at us!

[The dwarves look around suspiciously for Smaug. They exchange glances.]

DORI. Bilbo's right. We must move away from here. I feel as if his eyes were on the back of my head.

BOMBUR. It's a cold lonesome place. There may be drink, but I see no sign of food. A dragon would always be hungry in such parts.

OTHER DWARVES. Come on! Come on! Let us follow Balin's path!

1. Choose an exciting exchange in the story so far, perhaps between Bilbo and Gollum, Bilbo and Smaug, Thorin and the Goblin King, etc. Make it into a play scene. Use the sample above as a model for format and for ways of turning narration into drama.

Chapter 14

"Fire and Water"

Journal and Discussion Topics

1. What different interpretations did the townspeople make of the lights visible on the mountain?
2. Characterize Bard and the Master. What techniques does Tolkien use to encourage you to contrast the two men?
3. How is the setting of the town important in this chapter?
4. Was there any situational irony for you in this chapter? Any predictions fulfilled? Explain.
5. What motives guided the wood-elves' journey east?
6. What do you predict will happen in the next chapter? What indications do you have that this is possible?

Vocabulary

hotfoot: 246, in a hurry
huger: 246, more enormous
prophecies: 246, predictions about future
quench: 247, put out a fire
twanging: 247, ringing of a plucked string
heed: 247, attention
ablaze: 247, on fire
unquenchable: 247, unable to be put out
mirth: 248, gladness and laughter
gilded: 248, covered with gold
silvered: 249, appeared covered with silver
barb: 249, sharp projection from an arrow
shaft: 249, the long body of an arrow

throes: 249, pains
gledes: 249, archaic word; burning coals
waxing: 249, increasing in size (of the moon); opposite of waning
eminent: 251, most important
benefactors: 251, those who give benefits
imperishable: 251, never-ending
deposed: 251, removed from office
ample: 251, generous
recompense: 251, payment for services
strode: 252, p.t. stride; walked with long steps
contrived: 252, made happen with difficulty
array: 254, body of soldiers

Summary

The narrator flashes back two days to follow Smaug after he leaves the mountain. The people of Lake-town have observed lights near the mountain. Some think that the King under the Mountain is forging gold, but one grim man (Bard) thinks it is the dragon. Quickwittedly, he warns the Master and the alarms are sounded. The townspeople fill every available vessel with water, and the warriors arm as the dragon approaches. Because they have cut the bridges, the townspeople foil Smaug's first plan of attack. But, ignoring their arrows, he swoops down and sets the thatch roofs and wooden beam ends on fire. The women and children begin to get into boats, while men leap into the lake, and the Master prepares to flee in his gilded boat. Smaug, in the meantime, is planning how he will set the woods along the shore and the fields and pasture on fire and hunt down the boats. Now only one company of archers stands firm—those under Bard's leadership, but they, too, begin to flee. As Bard prepares his last arrow, the thrush suddenly appears and speaks to him. Bard can understand his language and hears him tell of Smaug's vulnerable spot. Invoking his last arrow, Bard shoots and hits the spot. Smaug falls, crashing upon the town and destroying it as he dies. Bard helps quell a movement to oust the Master and make Bard king. Instead he supports the Master by helping the townspeople and sending to the Elvenking for help, which is speedily sent. The townspeople build huts for winter shelter and, assuming that Thorin's company is dead, they prepare to march to the mountain and recover the now ownerless treasure.

Test: Chapters 10–14

Vocabulary

Look at each group of words. Tell why it is important in the story.

1. dire, devastating, ghastly _____

   _____

2. waterlogged, cramped, famished, buffeted _____

   _____

3. desolate, bleak, barren, desolation _____

   _____

4. quench, ablaze, gledes _____

   _____

5. stench, befouled, mouldered, charred, decay _____

   _____

Essay Topics

1. Pretend you are the Master. Write a monologue in which you clarify your reaction to the company when they first arrive.

2. Think of another story you know in which the leader is less worthy than one of his or her followers. Compare and contrast that leader and follower with the Master and Bard and with Thorin and Bilbo.

3. How do you think the company will respond to what has happened in Lake-town when they find out? What would you do if you were Thorin?

4. How did the slower pace of Chapter 11 make you feel as a reader?

5. What was your favorite part of the conversation between Smaug and Bilbo? Tell why.

6. What do you think Bilbo might do with the Arkenstone? Brainstorm at least four different answers and project the results if he did each.

7. Pretend you are Bard and you are telling your wife and children about the events of Chapter 14. Write the dialogue that you have with them.

Chapter 15

Journal and Discussion Topics

1. What role(s) have talking animals played in the plot of this story so far?
2. Bilbo thought "that the adventure was, properly speaking, over with the death of the dragon" and the narrator says he is wrong. What enemies might the company have? What do you think might happen?
3. What did the company do while they waited for the armies to approach?
4. How did Thorin react to the elves and men? How did the rest of the company feel? How do you know?
5. Compare and contrast the dwarves' song on pages 261–262 with their song on pages 13–15.
6. Bard and Thorin each present their view of the situation. How do you judge the situation?
7. What causes Thorin's hardness of heart?

Vocabulary

carrion: 255, those who eat the flesh of dead animals
coveted: 256, desired something very much, although belonging to another
breed: 256, a related group of animals
linger: 256, to be slow in departing
decrepit: 256, weakened by old age
alighted: 256, came to land
caper: 257, leap or prance about
amends: 257, compensation for an injury
wrung: 261, p.t. wring; to obtain as if by force

parley: 262, discussion with an enemy
descent: 263, coming from an ancestor
mingled: 263, mixed
reckon: 263, consider
kindred: 264, relatives
succoured/succored: 264, gave relief to
repent: 264, feel regret for
sires: 264, ancestors
besieged: 265, under siege
truce: 265, agreement to cease fighting

Summary

The narrator returns to Thorin and company and the large number of birds in the air. Bilbo spots the old thrush, who seems to be trying to communicate, but without success. After Balin mentions a raven named Carc, who helped the dwarves in time of need, the thrush hurries away and brings back Carc's son, Roäc, who informs the dwarves that Smaug is dead and warns them of the group of men and elves who are coming to seek the treasure. Roäc gives two pieces of counsel to the dwarves: don't trust the Master, but put faith in Bard; and, peace will cost them gold. Thorin rejects Roäc's advice and sends him to bid Dain, Thorin's cousin, to come to the company's assistance. The dwarves fortify the main entrance and send Fili and Kili out to find the ponies and bring supplies. The men and elves arrive and set up camp. Thorin challenges them, but receives no reply, and the dwarves sing a war song. The next morning, Bard comes for a parley and asks for recompense to Lake-town for the suffering caused by the dragon. Thorin is unmoved and says he won't make any deals while surrounded by armed warriors. When a messenger from the elves and men comes back later, Thorin shoots an arrow into his shield, and the messenger declares the mountain besieged.

Chapter 16

"A Thief in the Night"

Journal and Discussion Topics

1. Why do you think Tolkien might have called the chapter "A Thief in the Night" instead of "A Burglar in the Night"?
2. How does Thorin react to Roäc's advice?
3. Read to the bottom of page 268. What do you think Bilbo is going to do with the Arkenstone?
4. What motivates Bilbo to give the Arkenstone to Bard and the Elvenking?
5. Why do you think Bilbo shudders when he hands Bard the stone?
6. What motivates the Elvenking's reaction to Bilbo?
7. Do you think the Elvenking's prediction about Thorin's reaction will prove to be correct? Why or why not?

Vocabulary

bade: 266, p.t. bid; ordered or requested
unto: 266, for
avenged: 266, took vengeance on
lest: 266, for fear that
besets: 266, troubles; hems in
hastening: 267, going quickly
daresay: 267, think it's probable

siege: 267, surrounding a city or fortress to force a surrender
rouse: 268, awaken
recapture: 268, find again
sentinels: 269, guards
comely: 271, beautiful/handsome
thrice: 271, three times
brewing: 272, in the process of forming

Summary

The dwarves spend a lot of time searching for the Arkenstone, which Bilbo keeps hidden, and the ravens bring news that Dain and 500 dwarves are 2 days' march away. Bilbo decides that he must act. He offers to take over from Bombur who is standing guard, then promptly leaves the mountain and goes down to the elves and men. He demands to see the Elvenking and Bard. He presents them with the Arkenstone as a bargaining tool, explaining that he wants to avoid a war. This earns him the Elvenking's respect. Suddenly, Gandalf appears and congratulates Bilbo on his actions. Bilbo returns to the dwarves in time to wake Bombur for the changing of the watch.

Strategy 16

Theme

Directions:
Read the explanation, then answer the question.

The **theme** of a story might be thought of as the story's point or its message. A theme is often a generalization about life or human behavior or values—true, but not a truism—an author's insight into the way things work that he or she wants to share with readers. Theme is an important part of a story's meaning and is developed throughout the story. And it is important to note that a story can have multiple themes and meanings.

The message of a story is shaped by the author's intention and purpose. Besides patterns in the story (which often point to the theme), there are certain parts of a story that often refer to the theme: the title, the beginning, and the very end. An important character's first and final words are also likely to carry powerful indications of theme.

A persuasive or didactic piece of writing (such as a fable) might have an explicit moral—a clear statement of theme. Such a statement limits the interpretation of the piece. However, a piece of writing that was written with experience or aesthetic response in mind is more open to interpretation. Certainly the author may have a theme or themes in mind, but the readers bring their own insights and in this case different readers may legitimately find different meanings based on patterns and messages in the text combined with their own interpretations and insights. We seek for a balance between what is the text and what the reader brings to the text.

In a story, such as *The Hobbit*, that has a double plot—the story of Bilbo's interior journey and the literal journey of the company—you may find multiple themes. But also try looking for a joining of the plots with a single, over-arching theme.

1. State the theme or themes you find as you finish reading the story. Explain how you concluded that these statements are thematic.

Writer's Forum   A Possible Ending

The end of a book needs your close attention because it usually is meant to provide any needed explanation, to put a final exclamation point on the themes, and to leave the characters in a situation of equilibrium, noting what has happened to all the important characters. It should send the reader off feeling that all loose ends have been tied up. The ending should make sense of the foreshadowings and plot developments that have occurred so far in the book, and play out the main ideas that have been treated in the book so far.

1. Write an ending for the Hobbit picking up after Chapter 16 ends on page 272. Do not look ahead in the book as you do this.

Chapter 17   "The Clouds Burst"

Journal and Discussion Topics

1. Summarize the events of the battle.
2. What powers does Gandalf have in the battle? What powers does he lack?
3. What role does Bilbo have in the war?
4. What do you think the eagles' arrival signifies? What do you think will happen now that the eagles have arrived?

Vocabulary

embassy: 273, messengers between groups
casket: 273, small jewel box; fancy coffin
idle: 273, worthless
aloft: 274, in the air
stricken: 274, overcome so as to be
heirloom: 274, object of special value passed from generation to generation
league: 274, association
literally: 275, actually
forbear: 275, hold back from doing a thing
redeem: 275, buy back
deceit: 276, trick
hauberk: 276 a tunic of mail armor
mesh: 276, netting
mattocks: 277, digging tools with axe
plaited: 277, braided
flank: 278, right or left side of an array of soldiers

tarry: 278, wait
reconciliation: 278, renewal of a friendship
dread: 279 great fear
dominion: 279, kingship
assault: 280, attack
vanguard: 281, troops in front of the main body of the army
rent: 281, p.t. rend; pierce with sound
feint: 281, pretend display
wielding: 282, carrying ready for use
precipice: 282, cliff with a steep drop off
ravening: 282 destroying & eating greedily
scimitars: 282, swords with curved blades
bay: 282, unable to retreat
hemmed: 283, surrounded
hurtling: 285, moving with great speed

Summary

The dwarves are surprised to see an embassy including Bard, the Elvenking and an old man. The old man holds up the Arkenstone, and Thorin is stunned into silence to see his dearest treasure in their possession. When Thorin accuses the elves and men of theft, Bilbo admits his part. Thorin explodes with rage and wishes for Gandalf so he can curse him, and at this moment, the old man reveals himself as Gandalf. Only then will Thorin give Bilbo a chance to explain himself. But the explanation does no good. Thorin threatens Bilbo with death if he doesn't leave immediately, and while he says he will reclaim the Arkenstone with gold and silver, at the same time, he is secretly plotting to steal it back. Bilbo cries farewell and says, "We may meet again as friends," but Thorin threatens to shoot him. Dain arrives with his troops and challenges the elves and men. Bard wants to set upon them at once, but the Elvenking is reluctant to fight over gold. The dwarves mount an attack, but Gandalf intervenes, announcing the arrival of 2 more armies—the goblins and wolves. This news causes the Elvenking, Bard, and Dain to unite their forces. While Bilbo puts on his magic ring and hides, the 3 allied armies trap the goblins between two arms of the mountain and victory seems at hand, when suddenly other goblins overrun the mountain and come down upon them. Things are going badly for both Bard and the Elvenking, when they hear a trumpet call, and Thorin and company come out and rally the allies. But there are too few warriors. Just as it seems that the goblins must win the gate, Bilbo spots the eagles winging their way to the allies. At this moment a stone hurtles down and hits Bilbo's helm, and he is knocked unconscious.

Chapter 18   "The Return Journey"

Journal and Discussion Topics

1. How does Bilbo end up alone on Ravenhill?
2. What apology does Thorin make to Bilbo?
3. Why do you think Thorin calls Bilbo a thief, not a burglar?
4. Summarize the events that ended the war while Bilbo was unconscious. How do these events tie the episodes of the plot together?
5. How is the treasure divided in the end?
6. What pun does the Elvenking make in greeting Bilbo for the last time?
7. What change occurs in Bilbo as he travels home?

Vocabulary

notched: 287, with indentations
hoarse: 288, having a rough voice
stunned: 288, made senseless by a blow
mustering: 289, assembling a military group
dislodged: 289, removed from a position
fray: 289, fight

fugitives: 290, those fleeing to escape
perished: 290, died
slain: 290, killed
pursuit: 290, following in order to capture
abode: 291, place of residence; house
Yule-tide: 294, pagan mid-winter rite

Summary

When Bilbo regains consciousness, he is alone on Ravenhill. A man comes looking for him and takes Bilbo to the camp. Gandalf is delighted to see him and leads him to a mortally wounded Thorin, who apologizes for his words and actions. Bilbo tells Thorin that he is honored to have shared in the company's adventures, and Thorin, in a moment of truth, recognizes that Bilbo's values are higher than his own. Bilbo leaves and weeps in solitude. We find out that Fili and Kili are also dead. Then the narrator gives a flashback to explain the end of the battle. The eagles had drawn the goblins off the slopes so that the elves and men could rejoin the battle. But the allies were still outnumbered. Then Beorn arrived in his bear shape, took Thorin safely off the battlefield, and killed the Great Goblin. Coming back to the present, the narrator describes Thorin's burial under the mountain with the Arkenstone on his breast and Orcrist on his tomb. Dain becomes King under the Mountain, and the treasure is divided in a way that satisfies all. Bilbo does not talk much. Balin is the one to give Bilbo a parting greeting, and Bilbo invites the dwarves to stop in for tea if they are ever in his neighborhood. Bilbo makes a gift to the Elvenking in payment for the food and drink he stole. In return, the Elvenking names Bilbo an elf friend. Gandalf returns with Bilbo and they have adventures that are not detailed. They stop at Beorn's, and as they continue on the journey, the narrator says that the Tookish part of Bilbo is wearing out and the Baggins part is gaining strength.

Strategy 17 The Hero's Journey

*Directions:
Read the expla-
nation, then
answer the ques-
tion.*

Mythology expert Joseph Campbell characterizes the hero's journey as having a set pattern on which a myriad of variations are played out. The hero leaves his ordinary life on a journey into a region where he confronts the supernatural. He wins a victory and returns to the world he left a changed person. Not every stage is present in every story.

1. Read each summary of a stage in the hero's journey that is present in *The Hobbit*. Explain how each stage is present in Bilbo's story.

Departure
I. The Call to Adventure
The hero can enter into the adventure by mistake, or by being called by a herald who summons the hero. The call comes at a time when the hero is ready for inner growth. The hero's focus shifts from home to a distant place.

II. The Refusal of the Call
The hero is not always eager to assume the adventure offered. The hero has the opportunity to reject the call. If the hero refuses, his or her life may enter a state of paralysis until something happens to release him or her.

III. Supernatural Aid
The hero encounters a helper as the journey begins, a guide and protector (often an old woman or old man) who provides special powers to keep the hero safe in his or her encounters with evil. This protector usually appears to one who has already accepted the call, but not always. In fairy tales, the helper is often a wizard, hermit, smith, or shepherd.

IV. The Crossing of the First Threshold
The hero, accompanied by the guide, goes beyond the boundaries of his or her everyday life, enters the wilderness, and has a first encounter with the dangerous forces of the unknown.

V. The Belly of the Whale
The hero is swallowed up by the unknown.

Initiation
VI. The Road of Trials
The hero undergoes a series of trials often on a perilous journey. The guide or other helpers support him. Each trial may bring new insight. Victories may be repeated, but are not lasting.

Return
VII. The Magic Flight
The hero's return to the world from which he or she came accompanied by his or her guardian.

VIII. The Crossing of the Return Threshold
The hero leaves the realm of the unknown and returns from the dark to the light. The transition is not easy.

IX. Master of the Two Worlds
The hero, through the journey, has won the ability to pass back and forth from one world to the other.

X. Freedom to Live
The hero can now live with new freedom as a result of the journey, having matured and grown.

Chapter 19

"The Last Stage"

Journal and Discussion Topics

1. Compare and contrast the elves' songs on pages 295–296 with the dwarves' songs throughout the book.
2. What do you think Bilbo means when he says, "our back is to legends"?
3. Compare and contrast the journey towards adventure with the journey home.
4. What does Bilbo's poem reveal about him?
5. What is ironic in Bilbo's homecoming?
6. Would you say Bilbo's homecoming is heroic? Explain your answer.
7. What does it mean to say that Bilbo had "lost his reputation"?
8. How did his adventure change Bilbo?
9. What did Bilbo learn from Balin's and Gandalf's visit?
10. Why does Bilbo find the prophecies hard to believe? How does Gandalf respond?

Vocabulary

brink: 295, edge
cherish: 295, hold dear
lore: 297, traditional knowledge
jest: 298, gaiety
auction: 301, selling objects for highest bid
commence: 301, begin
presumed: 301, thought to be

extravagant: 302, beyond actual value
extensive: 302, having a wide range
refounded: 303, re-established an institution
prosperity: 303, being economically successful
sole: 303, alone; only

Summary

As Bilbo and Gandalf come to Rivendell, they hear the elves singing a song that contrasts the things that perish (the dragon, swords, crowns, strength, and wealth) with things that continue (nature, the elves) and contrasts the beauty of nature with the inferior qualities of wealth. After leaving the elves, they recover the troll gold. On the day they get their first sight of Bilbo's own hill, Bilbo suddenly stops and recites a poem that unites the Tookish and Baggins parts of himself. Gandalf responds, "You are not the hobbit that you were." At the door of Bilbo's house, they discover that Bilbo has been declared "presumed dead" and an auction of his household furnishings is underway. So Bilbo ends up buying back a lot of his own furniture. Bilbo finds that he has lost his silver spoons . . . and his reputation. He spends his time writing poetry and visiting elves. He is writing his memoirs one evening (which, it seems, have become the book we've been reading: *There and Back Again*), when Gandalf and Balin appear at the door. Balin reports that Bard has rebuilt Dale and that Lake-town has been refounded and now prospers. The three allies—men, elves, and dwarves—continue their friendship. The old Master, victim of the gold lust, has died in the wilderness. And the story ends with the paradox that Bilbo—a very little fellow—has had a hand in making prophecies come true in the world.

Writer's Forum

Poetry

Poet W. H. Auden spoke of poetry as a "game of knowledge, a bringing to consciousness, by naming them, of emotions and their hidden relationships." And thinking of poetry as a game we play with the poet can help us understand a genre that no one can clearly define.

The poet gives us sounds and sense set in a shape on a sheet of paper. The sounds include rhythms and repetitions. Saying the poem aloud several times will help you find its sound. The sense includes literal and figurative language, imagery, made-up words, onomatopoeia, double meanings and constructions that break the rules we usually follow for using language. The shape on the page helps us know how to read the poem. We enter the game and see what happens; we play with the sense and sound to not only find, but also to FEEL meaning.

One important element of a poem is the relationship between the sound and the sense, and this relationship is unique, depending on the subject of the poem and the speaker. The poet may be, but often is not, the speaker in the poem. If you examine the poems in *The Hobbit*, you will find that the speaker is one or more of the characters in the book, a persona, not a real person. If you say aloud the goblin songs on pages 60–61 and pages 105–106, the elvish songs on pages 48–49, pages 181–183, and pages 295–298, the dwarvish songs on pages 12–15 and pages 261–262, and Bilbo's song on page 300, you will find that the songs sound very different—the vowel and consonant combinations in the words, the accents, the rhythm and meter are connected in each case to the meaning, and to the minds and hearts (if goblins have hearts) of the characters who are the speakers.

1. Write a poem for the goblins, elves, dwarves, or any other character(s) in the book. Pick a particular time and place in the book that the poem responds to. If you wish, you may copy the rhythm and meter of one of the poems in the book, or you may create your own. Try to think the way the speaker you have chosen might think, and try to connect sound and sense.

Writer's Forum

Compare and Contrast a Book and a Movie

In a compare and contrast essay, you show the similarities and differences between two people, things, ideas, approaches, etc., and draw some conclusion based on this examination. You choose the categories to compare and contrast based on your purpose, and these categories will change depending on your topic.

Sometimes you will want to compare and contrast two different treatments of the same subject in different genres or media. You might want to do this if one work has been adapted or translated to create a new work, if a work has inspired or influenced another work, or if they have the same subject and enough in common or such wide differences that you think it would be fruitful to see the similarities and differences in how they make meaning and achieve their effects.

In this particular case, you are going to contrast the book of *The Hobbit* with the animated movie made from the book. Usually it is easier to do this if you both read the book twice and watch the movie at least twice, once to experience it, and once to take notes for your paper. Here are some questions that would be useful to examine:

- A movie is usually no longer than 2 hours, so a movie adaptation of a book leaves out material included in the book. What is excerpted or compressed in this movie?
- A movie script may have additional material not included in the book, or may make changes in the book. What additions and/or changes do you notice?
- How did your imaginings of the characters, settings, and actions of the book differ from the way they were presented in the movie? Compare the characterizations and the plots carefully.
- Apart from the book, did the movie work as an experience in itself? Did it hold your interest? Was it worthwhile?
- Did the theme(s) you identified in the book come out in the movie? If not, what message(s) did the movie give?
- Which did you like better—the book or the movie? Why?

Source words that can help you express concepts of similarity and difference include the following:

- as well as
- similarly
- differ
- whereas
- however
- likewise
- alike
- while
- but
- on the contrary
- at the same time
- resemble
- conversely
- though
- on the other hand

1. Write an essay comparing and contrasting the book and the movie of *The Hobbit*.

Vocabulary

Look at each group of words. Tell why it is important in the story.

1. descent, sires, kindred _____

_____

2. siege, recapture, sentinels _____

_____

3. assault, vanguard, embassy, flank _____

_____

4. perished, slain _____

_____

5. prosperity, refounded _____

_____

Essay Topics

1. The last words spoken by a character in a story are often significant. Tell your impressions of the last words of Thorin and Gandalf.

2. How has reading *The Hobbit* made a difference to you? What do you think you will remember most about it in the days ahead?

3. Did you find the ending satisfactory? Why or why not?

4. Compare and contrast Thorin and Smaug.

5. What was your favorite part of the book? Tell why.

6. Write your reaction to this statement of Tolkien's: "The Quest of the Dragon-gold [is] the main theme of the actual tale of *The Hobbit* . . ." (p. 159, Letters)

7. Write your reaction to this statement of Tolkien's: "Nowhere is the place or nature of 'the Wizards' made fully explicit. Their name, as related to Wise . . . is used throughout as utterly distinct from Sorcerer or Magician. It appears finally that they were as one might say the near equivalent in the mode of these tales of Angels, guardian Angels. Their powers are directed primarily to the encouragement of the enemies of evil, to cause them to use their own wits and valour, to unite and endure." (Letters, p. 159)

8. On page 302, it says that Bilbo is writing his memoirs, *There and Back Again*. What conclusions do you draw from this?

Answer Pages

Strategy 1: Beginning a Book, pages 10–11

Answers will vary. Allow for individual opinion.

1. Answers will vary.
2. Students may predict that a "hobbit" takes a journey and returns to where he began.
3. Possible responses: The character in front looks like a medieval peasant: he carries a sword; has his left hand in his pocket; he looks wary and well-fed. The character in back looks evil and resembles a space alien: pointed ears, pupil-less eyes, hooked nose, prominent teeth; appears to have no clothes—may not be civilized. Setting appears subterranean.
4. # of years since 1937.
5. Answers will vary.
6. Possible response: Some chapter titles suggest rest and comfort; others suggest trials or conflicts; it seems like an adventure.
7. The last two chapter titles suggest that the Hobbit returns safely from the journey.
8. Possible response: IV or V.
9. To find out what Bilbo Baggins has gained by the end of the book.
10. He seems friendly, responsive to the reader's imagined question, "What is a hobbit?" and addresses reader as "you." He uses a conversational tone, "As I was saying." He seems to know all about the world of the story and its inhabitants, and he seems to tell the truth, as tone and style indicate.
11. Bilbo, because he is referred to as "our particular hobbit" and the story is characterized as the "story of how a Baggins had an adventure. . . ."
12. In an imaginary world created by the author.
13. Imaginary creatures (hobbits and dwarves are mentioned) and an imaginary setting suggest fantasy.
14. Answers will vary. The narrator's comment about what the hobbit "gained" on his journey, may indicate a theme of a metaphorical, interior journey.
15. Possible response: Something will happen that will jar Bilbo into action from his present "immovable" state.
16. Answers will vary.

Chapter 1, "An Unexpected Party," page 12

1. Answers will vary. Possible responses: Which side of Bilbo's nature will win the struggle? Can Bilbo become a burglar and help the dwarves recover their treasure? Evidence includes Gandalf's prediction and defense of it; the struggle throughout the chapter of Bilbo's Tookish nature trying to come out; the title, the table of contents, the back blurb, the first sentence of Chapter 1, the last sentence of the first paragraph on page 2. Some students may say that there is a double focus, with the dwarves' goal of regaining their treasure also being of central importance.
2. "Interesting." It's the only word beginning with "inter-" that fits the context. The suppression of the "Tookish" idea models the interior conflict Bilbo is undergoing as the two sides of his nature compete for dominance.
3. A dragon named Smaug killed most of the dwarves and claimed their treasure.
4. It awoke the Tookish part of his nature and made him wish to travel and have adventures.
5. The claim, as the narrator says, is clearly hyperbole. Evidence for it is Bilbo's speech when he rejoins the company: "But treat it as the right one." Evidence against is Bilbo's generally timid nature and obvious fear.
6. Possible response: Gandalf is claiming that he has special foresight or knowledge that allows him to see a potential for burglary and adventure in Bilbo that neither the dwarves nor Bilbo can see.
7. No. Evidence includes "He turned with mock-politeness to Bilbo."
8. Possible response: Yes, because the Tookish side of his nature is awakened; he has responded to the dwarves' music, and their music is the last thing he hears before sleep; Gandalf seems to be ready to insist on it; Thorin has finally acknowledged Bilbo's role: "Before *we* go, I suppose you mean?. . . Aren't you the burglar?"
9. Possible responses: A group seeking to recover lost treasure; a person who has an internal struggle between wanting a safe, reclusive life and wanting a life of adventure; a dangerous journey undertaken with the aid of a wise guide; being surprised by a group of houseguests who are very demanding; the problem of finding the right person for an important job; trying to plan something with insufficient information.

10. The imaginary creatures—wizards, dwarves, dragons, hobbits—and magic.
11. Answers will vary. Students may tell the flashback information about the dwarves' treasure either as given or in chronological order.

Strategy 2: Plot—The Design of a Story, page 13

Answers will vary due to the dual nature of the plot. (Some students may focus on the internal conflict in Bilbo, and others may focus on the struggle to regain the dwarves' treasure. These two different perspectives will influence students to categorize the chapters differently.) In either case, students may recognize two crises because the event that insures the resolution of the struggle with Smaug for the dwarves' treasure is followed by another unexpected struggle among the five armies. The first crisis is in Chapter 12, "Inside Information," when Bilbo gets the information that makes Smaug vulnerable and that will allow the dwarves to recover their treasure. A second crisis occurs in Chapter 16, "A Thief in the Night," when Bilbo provides a way to break the deadlock between the dwarves and the rest of the peoples. The climax is in both Chapters 16 and 17, "The Clouds Burst" and "The Return Journey," in which everything, both Bilbo's private gain and the treasure, may all be lost, and what follows is denouement. Though the eagles' coming at the end of "The Clouds Burst" is an intimation of the moment that makes the ending inevitable, it is actually Beorn's appearance, told in flashback in "The Return Journey" that ensures the victory of the men, elves, and dwarves.

Chapter 2, "Roast Mutton," page 14

1. Possible response: Bilbo starts the chapter in his dressing-gown—an outfit that is suitable only for wearing in the home. He ends up wearing a dwarf's hood and cloak for the journey, which may symbolize his becoming one of the group, allying his interests with the dwarves' adventure. That these clothes are too large for him may indicate symbolically that he has to "grow into" his new role.
2. There are foreign sights and sounds; unfamiliar landscape, including signs of evil in the architecture; an irregular life; danger; and demands placed upon him to act the part of a burglar with the requisite cleverness and stealth.
3. It suggests they're uncivilized, not part of society.
4. Gandalf's trick that kept the trolls talking until the sun turned them to stone.
5. Exasperation; not gratitude.
6. Thorin, especially, uses high, formal speech (see page 16) that is cultured, precise, and romantic. The trolls are informal, crass, rude, and vulgar.
7. Answers will vary. Students may wish to make 3-D models.
8. Whether to leave safely or to prove himself as a burglar by returning to the dwarves with a stolen object.
9. Possible response: They seem more carried away by the idea of recovering the treasure than dedicated to careful planning. Thorin only glances at the map before dismissing it (page 19); he ignores Gandalf's warning about the roads East (page 21); he suggests getting revenge on the Necromancer, which Gandalf indicates is absurdly unrealistic (page 25); although they know they will face at least a dragon, the dwarves are apparently traveling without weapons, unprepared for danger or conflict; they are careless in approaching the trolls (page 38).
10. He finds the key to the troll's cave, and this gains them food and weapons.
11. Answers will vary. Students may refer to Odysseus and the Cyclops, Polyphemus; to Finn MacCumal or MacCumhail; to Jack the Giant Killer stories; etc.

Strategy 3: Setting and Mood, page 15

Students should show awareness of the various uses of setting, noting, first of all, that the story starts with a setting that reveals quite a lot about Bilbo's character before we even know his name.

Strategy 4: Characterization, page 16

1. The trolls' appearance; the trolls' words; the narrator's words about the trolls; the trolls' actions; the trolls' interactions among themselves, with Gandalf, and with the hobbit and the dwarves; the trolls' thoughts; and the setting of their cave.
2. Possible response: A goofy character, clownish, neither important, nor serious; not a hero.

3. Possible response: In Chapter 1, "An Unexpected Party," he was: haughty to Bilbo (page 10); professorial (page 16); condescending to Bilbo (page 21); inattentive to others (page 19, page 21). In Chapter 2, "Roast Mutton," he was gracious to Bilbo (page 29); courageous with the trolls (page 39); respectful and appreciative to Gandalf (pages 43–44).
4. Possible response: He's bolder, more consistently Tookish, more dedicated to the group. It seems that his abilities are being sharpened with use.
5. Possible response: He seems to guide firmly, but not force; he seems to feel and act responsible for all the others and the success of their mission; he is clever, resourceful, careful, mysterious, courageous.

Chapter 3, "A Short Rest," page 17

1. Possible response: Bilbo's reaction shows his Tookish nature, especially his love of beauty, as well as his thoughtfulness—he has made some inferences based on the elves' song. Thorin seems disturbed by the song, and the dwarves as a group are too focused on their quest and their hunger to turn aside. Students' individual responses will vary.
2. It is the same day—midsummer's eve—and there is the same shape moon—crescent—shining when Elrond holds up the map as when the runes on the map were written, causing them to become visible.
3. The dwarves' greed concerns him. Students' personal responses will vary.
4. The cryptic message written in moon runes tells the company how to gain access to the secret door.

Writer's Forum: Compare and Contrast, page 18

Students may use the various techniques of characterization on page 16 as their categories of comparison. Students may also discuss allegiance to good or evil as a category. There is little description of the elves' physical appearance. Perhaps Tolkien felt that it is more interesting to describe the physical characteristics of loathsome trolls than of pleasant elves. Alternatively, Tolkien may be allowing each reader to visualize his or her own conception of what elves are like, unimpeded by the limitations of whatever description he could write.

Strategy 5: Rhetoric, page 19

1. Possible responses include the following: "making a noise like elephants," page 2; "behaved exactly like a second edition of his . . . father," page 3; "open the door like a pop-gun!" page 10; "While hammers fell like ringing bells," page 14; "as quick as water flows," page 50; "as kind as summer," page 51.
2. Possible responses: As long as anyone can remember; going beyond the established boundaries, usually without due forethought or preparation; to walk into a situation that later gives one grief—used when one is taking responsibility for involvement in what happened; in a difficult situation; got their attention; at the last possible moment before disaster struck; we'll be dead.

Strategy 6: Maps, page 20

1. The first map has East at the top, South to the right, West on the bottom, and North at the left. The second map has North at the top.
2. The first map is a blow-up of a region found in the upper right corner of the second map. The second map shows a larger area.
3. Students may suggest either the elf-path farther North in Mirkwood, or the Old Forest Road. Thorin suggests vaguely "going East" to Long Lake and following the River Running North to Dale (pages 20–21). The company could also travel north around Mirkwood and avoid the elves and spiders that live in the forest.
4. Possible Responses: "Over Hill and Under Hill" might be about crossing the Misty Mountains. "Queer Lodgings" could refer to Beorn, which looks like a house. "Flies and Spiders" could refer to encountering the spiders shown in Mirkwood. "On the Doorstep" might refer to being at Lonely Mountain at the secret entrance trying to get in.

Strategy 7: Runes, pages 21–22

[See page 21 for Rune alphabet]

1. *Why is the door size important?* Because it is relatively small, they can be sure that Smaug does not use it to enter and leave the mountain—it could provide a safe entrance.
2. *What would you need to know to identify Durin's Day?* On what day the last new moon of Autumn first appears in the sky and at what time both moon and sun would be visible.

Chapter 4, "Over Hill and Under Hill," page 23

1. They say the **first** moon of autumn; Durin's Day comes on the day of the appearance of the crescent of the **last** moon of autumn.
2. His comment that what you find when you search "is not always quite the something you were looking for" suggests that they are about to get an unpleasant surprise; he tells us Gandalf's thought that caves are seldom unoccupied; Gandalf questions how thorough Kili and Fili were, raising the suspicion that they weren't at all thorough; all the company knew that Fili and Kili were exaggerating how carefully they had checked the cave; the narrator then explains what makes caves dangerous.
3. His cry warns Gandalf, who is able to escape the goblins, killing several of them in the process.
4. Students should use the categories from **Strategy 4, Characterization, page 16**, to organize the information given about the goblins on pages 59–67 of *The Hobbit*. They should recognize that they are not household nuisances who cause mischief on a small order, as they are presented in some other works.
5. Possible response: He is formal, respectful, and untruthful. His phrase "truly hospitable mountains" might be read as irony or obsequiousness.
6. Drawings will vary.
7. Possible responses include: *Yell*, page 59; *chuckled, laughed, stony voices, sing, croak, flap*, page 60; *yammer, bleat, echoed, ugly laughter, stamped, clapped, swish, smack, quarreled*, page 61; *howl of rage*, page 63; *clashed their shields, shouted, poof, yells, jibbering, jabbering, growls, curses, shrieking, skriking, a voice fierce and quiet*, page 64; *noises, cries*, page 66; *hardly any more noise than bats, shouted*, page 67. Onomatopoetic words might include: *clap, snap, clash, crash, crush, smash, swish, smack, crack, yammer, bleat* in the goblins' song on pages 60–61.
8. Possible response: "before you could say *rocks and blocks*"; "before you could say *tinder and flint*" (pages 59–60).
9. Answers will vary.

Strategy 8: Point of View, page 24

1. Possible responses include: "Now you know enough to go on with," page 2; "which I have just described for you," "If you had heard only a quarter of what I have heard . . .," page 3; "Look at the map at the beginning of this book, and you will see the runes there," bottom of page 19; "I don't suppose you or I would notice anything . . .," page 34; "pretty fair nonsense, I daresay you think it," page 49; "You know how terrific a really big thunderstorm can be . . .," page 56.
2. There are many possible responses, including many places on pages 6–11, as well as page 18, page 20, page 26, page 28, page 36, page 48, page 50, page 57, page 59.
3. Passages include pages 71–72, page 73, page 75, page 78, page 81, page 85.
4. Possible response: He is intimately acquainted with even minute details. He more frequently relates Bilbo's thoughts than anyone else's, but he knows what others are thinking and feeling.

Strategy 9: Fantasy, page 25

1. Students should recognize the following characteristics (extrapolating from the text): **Wizards** have some foreknowledge, but it is incomplete; they can do some magic. They use persuasion rather than magic, when possible. They are wise, but they don't always share all they know. They are extremely involved in the affairs of the world. Students may wonder what Gandalf's great interest is in helping the dwarves recover their gold. Since Elrond has reservations about their motives, certainly Gandalf would. **Elves** seem more removed from the world than wizards. They are merry and joyful and love the arts, especially singing, story-telling, and dancing. No evil can approach their secret sanctuary.

2. Answers will vary, depending on the book the student chooses. Possible titles are:
Trolls (ogres are the equivalent):
Three Billy Goats Gruff
D'Aulaires' Trolls by Edgar Parin and Ingri D'Aulaire
A Book of Ogres and Trolls by Ruth Manning- Sanders

Dwarves:
Snow White and the Seven Dwarfs (Grimm)
The Dwarfs (Grimm)
The Yellow Dwarf
Snow-White and Rose-Red

Test: Chapters 1–4, page 26
Vocabulary
1. Possible response: These words describe Bilbo's agitation at being faced with the prospect of an adventure, not to mention all the unexpected visitors in his house.
2. Possible response: These words are some of those used to describe the shrill, disturbing noises made by the goblins.
3. These are some of the old-fashioned words in the dwarves' song about gold.
4. Possible response: These are some of the pitfalls that the company faced while trying to locate Rivendell.
5. Possible response: These words are associated with the weapons found in the trolls' cave.

Essay Topics
1. Answers will vary. New predictions should be based on information in the first 4 chapters, as well as trends and patterns. Trends include the change in Bilbo toward being more Tookish. Patterns include Bilbo giving the company some help in each chapter; the company meeting a new group in each chapter, who either helps or hurts them; each chapter taking the company a step closer to accomplishing its mission.
2. Answers will vary. Students should discuss the character(s) chosen function in relation to the plot of the stories.
3. Answers will vary. Students may pick an adventure story in which treasure is sought (like *Treasure Island*), a journey story, either fiction or nonfiction (like *The Odyssey, Night Journey,* or *Homesick*) or a story about a metaphorical journey which represents internal development (like *The Maze in the Heart of the Castle*).
4. Answers will vary. Students should give cogent explanations.
5. Answers will vary. Students should give cogent explanations.
6. Answers will vary. Students' writing should accurately and consistently reflect their choice.
7. Answers will vary. Students should use 5 rhetorical figures in an accurate retelling.

Chapter 5, "Riddles in the Dark," page 27
1. His name comes from the horrid sound he makes when he swallows. He calls himself, "my precious."
2. Answers may vary. Students may raise the following points: Bilbo does not enter the contest willingly; he feels compelled and the stakes are very uneven, page 73; Bilbo does not trust Gollum to stick to the rules of the game and Gollum may not have entered into the game with a genuine intention to play by the rules, page 79; the last question was not a genuine riddle, page 79; the narrator states that Bilbo had won the game "pretty fairly," page 82; Gollum implicitly accepted Bilbo's question as fair when he guessed the answer to it, pages 78–79; Gollum makes 4 guesses, not 3 as agreed, pages 78–79.
3. He discovers that the dagger glows, acting as a goblin sensor, page 69. He begins to guess about the ring when Gollum runs past him after he falls, and Gollum then confirms the guess by his comments, which Bilbo overhears, pages 83–85.
4. Possible response: Gollum seems to believe Bilbo at first. But when he realizes that Bilbo has the ring, and remembers that Bilbo refused to tell what he **did** have in his pockets, he concludes that Bilbo is "tricksy." He immediately leaps to the conclusion that Bilbo is a generally "tricksy" character, and therefore, the type who would have lied from the outset.

5. Students may mention Bilbo's acquiescence to Gollum's suggestion that they play and to the stakes Gollum suggests; his last question in the riddle game; his thoughts about killing or wounding Gollum and his decision not to based on pity and compassion. Gollum plans to eat Bilbo almost as soon as he sees him. It is not clear that he ever intended to do anything else, even though he made the terms of the riddle contest that said that he would. Gollum seems to be under the control of the ring in some way. Other than that, he is motivated by hunger and "love" of the ring.

6. Answers will vary. Students should support their answers.

Strategy 10: Plot Conflict, page 28

1. Students may discuss Bilbo's internal struggle between his reclusive Baggins nature and his Tookish nature, the dwarves' quest for treasure, or both.

2. Possible responses:

1	Bilbo's two natures fight for dominance
2	Company vs. trolls
3	No major conflict
4	Company vs. goblins
5	Bilbo vs. Gollum (battle of wits)
6	Company vs. wargs and goblins
7	Gandalf vs. Beorn (battle of wits)
8	Company vs. spiders
9	Company (Bilbo) vs. wood elves (battle of wits)
10	No major conflict
11	Company vs. Lonely Mountain
12	Bilbo vs. Smaug (battle of wits)
13	No major conflict
14	Bard vs. Smaug
15	Company vs. men
16	Bilbo vs. the company or vs. his conscience
17	Men, elves, and dwarves vs. goblins, wargs, bats, and wolves
18	Bilbo's two natures reverse dominant roles
19	No major conflict

Chapter 7, "Out of the Frying-Pan into the Fire," page 29

1. Although he is horrified at the thought, Bilbo's conscience tells him that it is his duty to return to the goblins' realm and rescue his friends. Gandalf, likewise, feels that it is a duty to rescue Bilbo. The dwarves, however, are ready to leave Bilbo to the goblins and travel on without him. Students may conclude that compared to Gandalf and Bilbo, the dwarves are very self-centered, less developed morally, and have less compassion and loyalty to others beyond their own people.

2. Bilbo does not reveal that he has found the ring, and makes attendant changes in the story (e.g., "[Gollum] missed me in the dark") to cover the consequences of the ring's power of invisibility. Students may have different ideas about why Bilbo left things out. Possible responses: Especially after the praise he got for creeping into their midst unnoticed, Bilbo wants to make himself look like a capable and useful member of the party, so he tells the story in a way that makes himself seem clever and strategic; perhaps Bilbo is beginning to suffer from some of the possessiveness about the ring that Gollum displays, and wants to keep it to himself because it is gaining power over his mind. Students' answers about how they would have responded will vary.

3. Possible responses include: He is more flexible, more quick-thinking, more at ease, more capable of handling danger, more courageous, a more integral part of the company. Students may also say that he is more deceitful, citing the "unfair" ending of the riddle game and the concealment of the ring from the dwarves and Gandalf.

4. Their awe at Bilbo's success and particular interest in the riddle game may partly result from it being such a time-honored test.

5. Possible responses include the following: At first it is helpful: an avalanche helps them get down the

mountain quickly and a group of trees saves them from being crushed by the rocks. Then the trees provide a refuge from the wolves. But when the goblins plant the fire around the base of each tree, the trees become a trap. Finally, the eagle's eyrie, high in the mountains, provides a refuge. The last reference to setting in the chapter, Bilbo's dream of his house, shows a change or development in Bilbo's character by showing a sharp contrast between Bilbo's newfound comfort in the eyrie and his feeling of being displaced in his own home.

6. He has the narrator explain the origins of a proverb in Middle-earth—the saying, "Escaping goblins to be caught by wolves!", the origins of which he traces to the incident in this chapter.

Strategy 11: Foreshadowing and Flashback, page 30

1. Possible responses include: Dori's account of dropping Bilbo, page 92; Bilbo's account of his adventures in the goblins' realm, page 93; Gandalf's account of his actions after the goblins took the ponies, pages 94–95.
2. Possible responses include: "He may have lost his neighbours' respect, but he gained. . .," page 2; "You will have to manage without pocket-handkerchiefs, and a good many other things, before you get to the journey's end," page 30; Bilbo's change of clothes, pages 30–31; "I wish I was at home in my nice hole by the fire, with the kettle just beginning to sing!' It was not the last time that he wished that!", page 32; "[Gandalf] knew that something unexpected might happen, and he hardly dared to hope that they would pass without fearful adventure over those great tall mountains with lonely peaks and valleys where no king ruled. They did not," page 56; All the foreshadowing about the cave in Chapter 4 (see the answer to question 2 for **Chapter 4, "Over Hill and Under Hill," page 23.**); etc.

Chapter 7, "Queer Lodgings," page 31

1. Gandalf deceives Beorn about the number of people in the company. He goes to Beorn's house with only Bilbo and in telling the story, he changes the way he refers to the size of the group as more and more members appear, two by two, per Gandalf's instructions. Because of Beorn's interest in the story, he accepts a large number of guests, which he would otherwise have sent away.
2. At first Beorn is suspicious and gruff. When he hears that they have had trouble with goblins, he softens a little. When the dwarves begin to come in, he states that he is not "over fond" of them. But at Balin and Dwalin's appearance, he is amused. His pleasure at the story convinces him to give them dinner, although he is still suspicious. When checking reveals their story to be true, he offers them generous help and advice.
3. Students might use the following categories: hospitality; attitude towards dwarves; relationship to nature; help to the company; physical description.
4. He lends the dwarves ponies and Gandalf a horse; he gives them food, water skins, and bows and arrows; he gives them advice about their route, about avoiding the water and food in Mirkwood, and about straying from the path; he guards their journey up until their entrance to Mirkwood.
5. Gandalf says to Bilbo, "You have got to look after all these dwarves for me." Answers will vary about students' estimate of Bilbo's ability to do this. Some may trust in Gandalf's judgment; others may say that the evidence doesn't suggest that Bilbo has the capacity.

Strategy 12: Setting and Mood, page 32

Possible answers to setting and plot action. Answers for mood will vary.

1	Bilbo's house; tea party
2	The Lone-lands; capture by and escape from trolls
3	Rivendell; rest and Elrond reads runes
4	Goblin realm; capture by goblins and flight
5	Goblin realm; riddle contest; Bilbo's escape
6	Pine glade; attack by goblins and wargs; rescue by eagles
7	Beorn's home; rest and help (food, ponies, route) for further journey
8	Mirkwood; capture by and rescue from spiders
9	Wood-elves' palace; capture by and escape from wood-elves
10	Lake-town; rest and help for trip to Lonely Mountain
11	The doorstep to the Secret Door; the door is opened
12	Smaug's hoard; Bilbo steals cup; Bilbo learns of Smaug's vulnerable spot and so does the thrush; Smaug leaves to attack Lake-town, and the company hides in the mountain

13	Inside Lonely Mountain; Bilbo finds the Arkenstone; the dwarves arm themselves; the company journeys to a guardroom, where they make camp
14	Lake-town; the town is destroyed and Smaug dies
15	Lonely Mountain—the guardroom; the ravens take messages to Dain; the elves and men encamp before the mountain; Thorin refuses to share the treasure; the armies declare the mountain besieged
16	Encampment of elves and men; Bilbo gives Bard and the Elvenking the Arkenstone as a bargaining tool
17	Lonely Mountain; Thorin agrees to ransom the Arkenstone; Dain's army arrives and begins a battle with the elves and men; Gandalf intercedes and warns them that the goblins and wolves are coming; the goblins gain the upper hand; the eagles come
18	Lonely Mountain; Thorin makes peace with Bilbo and dies; Gandalf and Bilbo take their share of the treasure and leave for Hobbiton
19	Rivendell; Hobbiton; Gandalf and Bilbo visit the elves; they travel to Hobbiton; Bilbo is presumed dead, but is reinstated, having lost some spoons and his reputation; he visits elves and writes poetry and a memoir; Balin and Gandalf visit him

Writer's Forum: Diary Entry, page 33

The style of students' diary entries should show a connection with the content of the entries. The entries should have a consistent, well-developed, and recognizable point of view. The connection of the diary entry to the text should be evident.

Chapter 8, "Flies and Spiders," page 34

1. The setting creates continuous obstacles that interfere with the company's efforts to move along on their journey.
2. Answers should include: Bombur's fall in the river; the company's loss of hope; their inability to replenish the food supply (and thus, their attempts to join the wood-elves' feasts); the encounter with the giant spiders.
3. Possible answers include: Fighting with his sword; the invisibility granted by the ring; the element of surprise; spying in enemy territory; throwing stones; leading the spiders away from the dwarves; teasing them by name-calling; making himself a moving (not stationary) target; adapting his plans to circumstances (dropping everything to save Bombur).
4. Possible response: It is like a rite of passage; he comes to believe for the first time in his own power, his own capability to fend for himself without outside aid.
5. He tells them about the ring's power of invisibility. He wants to draw the spiders away so that the dwarves can escape, but in order for this to work, they must know what he's doing.

Strategy 13: Character, page 35

Answers will vary. Possible responses may include the following details:

generosity/selfishness: Bilbo increasingly takes risks out of generosity (not just to prove his abilities), whereas the dwarves are willing to give Bilbo up for lost rather than take a risk; Balin is more generous than the other dwarves, but as a group they are primarily focused on their own agenda; at the end, Thorin's view undergoes a major revision and he comes to value Bilbo's perspective. The Master, although he holds a leadership role, does not exercise it with integrity because he is too selfish. He seems to use his power for his own benefit.

honesty/deception: Gollum seems to be honest only when forced to it by fear of the consequences; he seems to have reached the stage where he is convinced by his own self-deceptions (for example, about his birthday present, so-called); Bilbo tries to deceive Gandalf about his reaction to Gandalf's offer of an adventure and this seems to stem from immaturity; he deceives the dwarves and Gandalf about the ring in order to appear capable, but he gives up the deception when the situation demands it; he deceives Smaug into revealing his vulnerable spot; he deceives the dwarves about the Arkenstone in order to try to make peace; under the power of gold lust, Thorin is planning to deceive the elves and men about his intentions to ransom the Arkenstone.

uncertainty/self-confidence: At the beginning, the text shows a contrast between Gandalf's trust in Bilbo and Bilbo's uncertainty. Over the course of the book, Bilbo's self-confidence increases to the point at which he becomes the de facto leader of the company, aided partly by Gandalf's departure, as well as by his own growth.

leadership/abrogation of responsibility: Bilbo goes from wishing Gandalf were present to take over the responsibility for the company, to accepting his own leadership role. Gandalf delegates responsibility when other obligations call him from the company; Thorin abrogates responsibility in denying help to the men of Lake-town, in his treatment of Bilbo, and in his plan to steal the Arkenstone—he accepts it when he apologizes to Bilbo before he dies. The Master accepts responsibility when it means honors for him, and abrogates it whenever there is risk; his final abrogation ends in his death. In order to keep order in Lake-town, Bard takes on responsibility and leadership that rightly belongs to the Master, and his choice to do this results in the death of Smaug and an easier time for the townspeople.

Chapter 9, "Barrels Out of Bond," page 36

1. Possible response: The dwarves' were angry, impolite, and unwilling to communicate. This made him suspicious. They had also broken the law of his realm, according to his understanding, and they refused to explain.
2. At first he was aimless. Then he wished for Gandalf. Finally he realized that he was going to have to act himself if there was to be any chance of freeing the dwarves.
3. Possible response (students may differ on what they call luck; have them define their terms): Planning is responsible for finding the cells where the 12 dwarves were kept; luck is responsible for his overhearing the news of another dwarf—Thorin. Luck is responsible for Bilbo's discovery of the portcullis exit and for his knowledge of river trade. Planning is responsible for the overall shape of the plan. By luck he finds out that the chief of guards and king's butler will be drinking so that he may be able to steal the key. Planning is responsible for getting the dwarves safely packed. Luck is responsible for Bilbo himself getting out—he forgot to plan for that.
4. Possible points of comparison and contrast include: the strategies necessary (fighting is necessary against the spiders); the role of luck; the importance of planning; the risks in the two situations.
5. Possible points of comparison and contrast include: the sound; the points of reference; the language; the sentence length; the purpose; the poetic form.

Strategy 14: Irony, page 37

Answers will vary. Here are some examples of irony that students might note: the irony of Gollum unintentionally leading Bilbo to the backdoor, keeping a promise he had no intention of keeping, pages 84–87; the irony of Bilbo being forced to burgle in the wood-elves' palace, "I am like a burglar that can't get away, but must go on miserably burgling the same house day after day," page 173; the irony of Gandalf "turning up" just when Thorin wishes for him, page 274.

Writer's Forum: News Article, page 38

Students may choose for an audience the wood-elves, the dwarves, the townspeople of Lake-town, etc. The first paragraph should succinctly sum up the main information about the event, details should be presented in a reasonable order, and made-up facts should be consistent with the characters and situation. Made-up interviews should have characters speaking from an appropriate point of view, and capitalization and punctuation for quotations should be accurate.

Test: Chapters 5–9, page 38
Vocabulary

1. Possible response: These words describe the way Gollum moves.
2. Possible response: These words show Bilbo's initial misunderstanding about the nature of Beorn.
3. Possible response: These words are associated with the chief guard and the king's butler drinking together.
4. Possible response: These words are part of the setting in Mirkwood.
5. These words have to do with the eagles' abode.

Essay Topics

1. Possible responses:

   Mountain—"Roots" is used metaphorically, and "up, up it goes" means height, not movement.

   Teeth—"Horses" are teeth; the "red hill" is the gums or tongue; "champ" and "stamp" are chewing.

   Wind—Personification with regard to sound, movement, effect on people, and sound again.

   Sun on daisies— "Eye" is both sun in "blue face," sky; as well as daisy (here petals = lashes) in "green face," grass.

   Dark—Definition by negatives makes this one difficult; the places where it occurs are hard to connect. "It comes first" means prior to creation when God made light; "follows after" refers to the time after the end of the world. "Ends life" doesn't mean that it causes life to end, but that, people experience death and burial, literally and figuratively, as a descent into darkness. "Kills laughter" is also metaphorical, referring perhaps to fear of the dark.

   Egg—The "box" is the eggshell; the "golden treasure" is the yolk.

   Fish—"Without breath" refers to the fish's use of gills; fish are cold-blooded; "ever drinking" is figurative referring to the fish's environment, not its actual use of water in its diet; "mail" refers to its scales. Fish, table, man, stool, cat—clues reside in number of legs and physical relationship of elements; fish has no legs, small table has 1, man has 2, stool has 3, cat has 4.

   Time—Depends on a kind of personification that confuses the interpretation of *devours, gnaws, grinds, slays, ruins,* and *beats*.

2. Possible response: The spiders argue about how long to hang the dwarves before eating them and about whether they should be hung alive or dead. The dwarves are already hanging during the conversation. The goblins are just exploring gruesome possibilities in song, not arguing. The trolls are having a very heated argument about how to prepare and cook the dwarves and when.

3. Answers will vary. Explanations should be cogent.

4. Answers will vary. Students' stories should have an obvious and integral add-on element, but this element will vary—it could be added characters, objects, a plot sequence, etc.

5. Words include: *gloomy, light, little bright hole, dimness, glimmer, beam of sun, dark, pitch-dark, gleams, fade, shine, watch-fires, flicker, gloom.* Answers about the effects will vary. Students may mention the contrast between the warm, friendly light in Beorn's house and the dark of Mirkwood; that Mirkwood seems an apropos name; that the farther they go, the darker it seems to get; that the lack of light gives an air of foreboding; etc.

6. Answers will vary. Some students may connect the playful, unpresumptuous name with Bilbo's own name, the size of his sword, his character. Some may feel that a sword should have a more majestic name.

7. Quoits: A circle of rope or iron is thrown at an upright pin to ring it or come as close as possible. Dart-throwing: Small pointed missiles are thrown at a round target. Shooting at the wand: Archers shoot arrows at an upright wand 6" wide and 6' long from a distance of 100 yd. Bowls: Balls are rolled on a green at a target or group of targets. Ninepins: A bowling game

8. Possible responses include: "Gandalf thought of most things; and though he could not do everything, he could do a great deal for friends in a tight corner," page 65; "'Bother burgling and everything to do with it! I wish I was at home in my nice hole by the fire, with the kettle just beginning to sing!' It was not the last time that he wished that!" page 32; ". . . Bilbo never saw them again except high and far off in the Battle of Five Armies. But as that comes in at the end of this tale we will say not more about it just now," page 112; "The day will come when they will perish and I shall go back!", page 115.

9. Possible response: The dwarves have come to rely on Bilbo's skill and guidance and luck. Bilbo has (especially with the naming of Sting) begun to feel himself a leader/guide of the company, although Thorin still retains the status of elder.

Chapter 10: "A Warm Welcome," page 40

1. The escape from the wood-elves, although Bilbo didn't know it at the time, put the company on the only route that would lead them safely to their destination.

2. Students should describe how the dwarves looked, felt, and acted when Bilbo got them out of the barrels in the dark.

3. Students should mention the guards' initial surprise and consternation, the reaction of those who believed in the legends, and the captain's more measured reaction.

4. The Master was suspicious of the dwarves, hesitant, did not put stock in the old songs and legends, and was most interested in commerce and money.

5. Most enthusiastically embraced the company as fulfilling the prophecies of the return of the King under the Mountain, and the Master decided to go along with the majority.

6. He thinks that they intend to collect the treasure and return to whence they came, whereas they intend to renew their kingdom under the mountain.

7. Possible responses: The company came out of their barrels into cold water, hungry, thirsty, and greeted by no one. When they were brought to the Master's feast, the first response was that of the wood-elves, which was anything but warm. Students who have read ahead or know the story may suggest that it is ironic in the light of Smaug's fire-breathing later in the story, which could be called a "warm welcome" of a sort.

Chapter 11, "On the Doorstep," page 41

1. The setting creates obstacles to the accomplishment of the goal of entering Lonely Mountain.

2. The dwarves ignore what Elrond said and try first to identify the door and then to break it open—without success. Bilbo becomes lonely and weary. The dwarves become glummer and glummer.

3. Possible responses: Beorn's advice about not eating in Mirkwood (shooting the squirrel; trying to reach the wood-elves' feasts) and not straying off the path; Elrond's advice about the door; Gandalf's advice about *thoroughly* checking the cave in the Misty Mountains.

4. Possible response: Bombur says, "And the knotted ropes are too slender for my weight." The narrator adds, "Luckily for him that was not true, as you will see." Students' conclusions will vary.

5. The dwarves grow impatient and blame Bilbo for not getting in the door. They consider sending him around to the Front Gate, and this makes him miserable and unable to sleep.

6. Some students may think that the thrush knows something or is a portent of something.

7. Answers may vary. Students may talk about imagining what the passage describes, or feeling the flowing darkness.

Chapter 12, "Inside Information," page 42

1. Students' characterizations of Bilbo should include Bilbo's comments about himself, pages 210–211; the description of his descent down to Smaug, pages 212–213; Bilbo's cleverness and mistakes in his interview with Smaug, pages 221–225. Students' characterizations of the dwarves should include the information on page 211 about the dwarvish character; Thorin's steadiness in the face of danger, page 216; change in their attitude toward Bilbo, pages 218–219.

2. He is enchanted by the gold and desires to impress the dwarves. Some students may think that the second reason is an afterthought, and it may be.

3. Tolkien uses words, thoughts, appearance, actions, interactions, name, and chosen setting to reveal Smaug's character (see **Strategy 4: Characterization, page 16**). Students should expand on each of these.

4. Bilbo tries to trick Smaug into showing Bilbo his underside so that Bilbo can determine if Smaug is vulnerable. Bilbo flatters Smaug, and Smaug is, in fact, tricked into showing the hollow on his breast. Smaug tries to separate Bilbo from the company by raising his suspicions about the dwarves' intentions towards Bilbo. Smaug succeeds to a certain extent, but Bilbo exerts his will and keeps up "an effort to remain loyal to his friends." Afterwards, he repeats the episode to them, and Thorin addresses it directly, but Bilbo's reaction to Thorin's explanation is not given. Riddle-talk explanations: "I come from under the hill" (refers to his home, Bag-End); "and under the hills and over the hills my paths led" (refers to journey up Misty Mountains and through goblin's realm); "and through the air" (refers to transport by eagles); "I am he that walks unseen" (refers to ring of invisibility); "clue-finder" (may refer to opening the door); "web-cutter" (refers to his fight with spiders); "stinging fly" (refers to his dagger Sting and being prey of the spiders while fighting back); "lucky number" (refers to Gandalf's statement at the Tea Party—pages 18–19); "buries friends alive and drowns them and draws them alive from the water" (refers to escape from the wood-elves' realm in barrels); "I came from the end of a bag, but no bag went over me" (refers to his home, Bag-End); "friend of bears" (refers to relationships with Beorn); "guest of eagles" (refers to night spent in the eyrie); "Ringwinner" (refers to the riddle game with Gollum and the finding of the ring); "Luckwearer" (seems to be a general reference to Bilbo's good luck); "Barrel-rider" (refers to Bilbo's clinging to a barrel to escape from the wood-elves).

5. Possible responses: He underestimates Smaug's knowledge of his hoard and the intensity of Smaug's reaction to the missing cup; he forgets about a dragon's sense of smell and ability to sleep with half an eye open; he is so pleased with his riddling that he unintentionally gives Smaug a lead toward Lake-town; he underestimates Smaug's power to persuade him with dragon-spell; he mocks Smaug, again underestimating Smaug's reaction.

6. Bilbo is at first overwhelmed with it, and steals the two-handled cup under its influence. He is, however, able to separate himself from it, as on page 229. Smaug is so much under its spell that although the narrator suggests that he never before wanted or used the cup, he is willing to murder to recover it. The dwarves are enchanted by it, especially Thorin with the Arkenstone.

Strategy 15: Reference, Allusion, and Parody, page 43

1. Possible response: Smaug, like the Beowulf dragon, has stolen treasure from people and built up a treasure hoard. Bilbo, like the man in need, steals a cup, and takes it to the dwarves to make peace with them. Smaug, like the Beowulf dragon, smells the intruder upon awakening, and is immediately aware of the theft. Like the Beowulf dragon, Smaug vows to punish the thief, and (after an extra episode in *The Hobbit*) sets the town on fire. Like the Beowulf dragon, the killing of Smaug requires assistance (here from the thrush), but Bard, unlike Beowulf, does not die. The parody chiefly lies in the substitution of the "common man," Bilbo Baggins, for the great king and hero Beowulf; in the characterization of Smaug; and in the addition of dialogue.

Chapter 13, "Not at Home," page 44

1. As the chapter begins, the narrator and readers know that Smaug is "not at home," but the company does not.

2. Possible response: Bilbo assesses the situation, and sees that action must be taken. He has lost his fear, and is able to trust in his luck. Bilbo has enough courage to defy Smaug at the risk of his life and the inner resources to provide leadership for the dwarves, who only agree with his plan because they are desperate, and who, although they accompany him, are terrified, and are not willing to take any unnecessary risks.

3. Bilbo is drawn by the enchantment of the Arkenstone and "steals" it, but in general he is less affected than the dwarves, who are bewitched by the hoard and sigh over the treasure they cannot stuff into their pockets. Thorin hunts particularly for the Arkenstone without telling anyone.

4. Possible response: He is of two minds—he both enjoys the heroic appearance and fears that he is not the heroic type, and looks merely silly. This may be seen as a continuation of the Baggins/Took split in his personality.

5. The chapter begins with the claustrophobic terror of the tunnel. This is followed by the enchanting atmosphere of the treasure hoard (despite the dragon smell), and the journey through the mountain, which highlights the dragon's destruction, contrasting with the enduring beauty of the dwarvish architecture, and nature.

6. They are hiding out in a guardroom, well away from Smaug's chamber, but they do not know where Smaug is or what he is doing, and this makes them uneasy about their situation.

Writer's Forum: A Scene from a Play, page 45

Students' scenes will vary. Scenes should combine stage directions and dialogue in an appropriate format. The choices made to transform narration into drama should be defensible.

Chapter 14, "Fire and Water," page 46

1. Some of the townspeople think that the King under the Mountain is forging gold and that the river is running gold from its source under the mountain. One man (Bard) thinks it is Smaug's fire.

2. Possible response: The narrator makes it clear that it is Bard's urging, not the Master's, that gives the townspeople the strength to fight Smaug. The narrator juxtaposes the description of the Master, about to desert the town and interested only in saving himself, with that of Bard, holding the last company of archers in place by his will and courage, and saving lives by destroying Smaug.

3. Students should recognize the specific setting of the town as integral to the battle, both in terms of strategy and outcome.

4. Students may find situational irony in the mistaken idea of the townspeople that the King under the Mountain is forging gold, when what they actually see is Smaug. Some students may feel irony when Bard refuses to become king, because they think that this would be fitting. Some students may have predicted that Bilbo's knowledge of Smaug's vulnerable spot would somehow be valuable, and some may have noticed that the thrush seemed to understand Bilbo's report of his conversation with Smaug.
5. They want a share in Smaug's wealth, but they also pity the townspeople.
6. Predictions will vary. Students should support their predictions with evidence from the book.

Test: Chapters 10–14, page 47
Vocabulary
1. These words describe Smaug.
2. These words tell of the condition of the dwarves upon getting out of the barrels after their escape from the wood-elves' realm.
3. These words describe the landscape approaching Lonely Mountain.
4. These words relate to the fire Smaug set in Lake-town.
5. These words describe the setting that Thorin and company passed through on their journey from the treasure hoard to the guardroom where they went for safety. They show the disintegration of the castle due to Smaug.

Essay Topics
1. Answers will vary. Students should characterize the Master in a way that is consistent with the story.
2. Answers will vary. Stories with tyrants are possible choices, such as Prince John and Robin Hood. Students should clearly identify the categories on which they base their comparison.
3. Students may recognize that the dwarves' greed will encourage them to be selfish, or they may think that the dwarves' characteristic selfishness will be transformed as their attitude towards Bilbo has been transformed. Either position is supportable. Personal responses will vary.
4. Answers will vary. Students may appreciate the change of pace as representative of the change of pace for the characters in the story or they may find it tedious.
5. Answers will vary. Students should clearly identify the portion of the conversation and their reasons for choosing it.
6. Answers will vary. Possible responses: Give it to Thorin at a chosen time in order to gain some favor; ask for it as his portion of the treasure; give it to the people of Lake-town to help them; steal it.
7. Dialogues will vary. Students should convey the characterization of Bard given in the story, but allow for some softening and lighter touches, given the context of the dialogue.

Chapter 15, "The Gathering of Clouds," page 48
1. Students should mention Beorn's animals, the wargs, the thrush, and the ravens in their answers.
2. Answers will vary. Students may realize that through Elrond and Beorn, questions have been raised about the dwarves' lust for gold and questions have also come up about the contrast between the dwarves' values and those of Bilbo and others.
3. They fortify the main entrance and build a new path. They also sing a war song.
4. Thorin refuses to share the treasure, which he says no one has a claim to. He considers the elves and men as foes and thieves because they are armed. Bilbo had thought that Thorin would admit the justice of the claim and share the gold. Most of the other dwarves agree with Thorin, except Bombur, Fili and Kili, and these three do not dare to express their views.
5. Students may consider that the later song has a different tone—it is threatening and defiant, rather than nostalgic and seeking restoration.
6. Most students will probably consider Bard to be more fair.
7. According to the narrator, it is the power of gold.

Chapter 16, "A Thief in the Night," page 49
1. Possible response: He might have done it to distinguish Bilbo's actions here from his work in the dwarves' employ as their burglar.
2. He ignores it.

3. Answers will vary. Possible responses: use it to bargain; give it to the elves and men.
4. Bilbo gives it to them to aid them in their bargaining with Thorin.
5. Possible response: Bilbo may have shuddered because he realized the magnitude of what he was doing—not only acting alone without counsel and putting himself at Thorin's mercy, but also giving up a most beautiful and splendid treasure.
6. Possible response: He is amazed by Bilbo's willingness to take an enormous personal risk for the sake of justice; he is surprised that Bilbo does not share the dwarves' ethics.
7. Possible response: The Elvenking assumes that Thorin will not value Bilbo's choice and implies that Thorin may not honor and welcome Bilbo's return. There is good evidence to support this conclusion: Thorin's singular attachment to the Arkenstone; his previous refusal of advice from Roäc; his relatives' fear of disagreeing with him.

Strategy 16: Theme, page 50

Answers will vary. Students may refer to Thorin's last words or Gandalf's last words, or to the description of Bilbo on page 302.

Writer's Forum: A Possible Ending, page 51

Answers will vary. Students' endings should provide a conclusion for the balance of Took and Baggins in Bilbo's personality; tell whether and how Bilbo returned home and what (if anything) he gained; tell how the interactions of the dwarves, elves, and men concluded and how the treasure was divided.

Chapter 17, "The Clouds Burst," page 52

1. Students should include the main details of the battle.
2. Gandalf is able to bring the men, elves, and dwarves into an allegiance. He is able to come up with a good, strategic plan. It seems that he was going to do a blast of magic when all seemed lost, but he does not seem able to work miracles or win the battle for the allies. He is wrong in the timing of the arrival of the goblins, wolves, wargs, and bats.
3. Bilbo puts on his ring and sits out the war.
4. Possible answer: It may signify a change in the balance of power between the allies and their foes, suggesting that the tide may turn against the goblins.

Chapter 18, "The Return Journey," page 53.

1. He was wearing the magic ring, so the searchers who sought him could not see him.
2. Thorin recants his words and actions at the Gate and acknowledges that Bilbo's values are superior to his own.
3. Answers will vary. Thorin may be giving Bilbo more elevated status, since *burglar* may connote a household criminal and *thief* a more lofty and adventurous criminal.
4. Students should mention the appearance of characters met previously on the journey to the Lonely Mountain—eagles, Beorn, the goblins, and the wargs— and note that the recollection of many episodes of the journey gives a unity to the plot.
5. One fourteenth goes to Bard to ransom the Arkenstone, and Bard shares with his friends and followers, the Master of Lake-town, and the Elvenking. Bilbo gets two small chests, one filled with gold and the other silver, although Dain offers him more. The Arkenstone is buried with Thorin.
6. He says "may your shadow never grow less," meaning both, "may you stay healthy and hearty," and "may you not become even more difficult to see, making it all the more easy for you to steal."
7. The balance between the Took part of him and the Baggins part is moving towards a new equilibrium in which the Baggins part holds a larger place.

Strategy 17: The Hero's Journey, page 54

Possible responses:

I. Gandalf calls Bilbo by inviting him to share Thorin and company's adventure.
II. Bilbo refuses the call by going inside and giving Gandalf an insincere invitation to tea.
III. Gandalf is the protector and guide for Bilbo's journey.
IV. The first threshold is the Lone-lands and the encounter with the trolls.

V.   Bilbo descends into the Misty Mountains to the realm of the goblins.
VI.   The trials include fighting the spiders, the escape from the wood-elves, and the encounters with Smaug.
VII.   Bilbo begins his return home, accompanied by Gandalf.
VIII.   Bilbo is sought out after the battle is over and makes his final use of the magic ring for heroic deeds, returning to the world of the visible.
IX.   Bilbo returns home, but his poem shows the integration of his Tookish and Baggins sides and his visits to elves show that he can still cross into the other world.
X.   Bilbo's new freedom is expressed in the description of him on page 302.

Chapter 19, "The Last Stage," page 55

1. The elves contrast the things that perish (dragon, sword, throne, crown, strength, and wealth) with things that last (grass, leaves, flowing water). They then contrast stars and gems; the moon and silver; fire and gold—three elements of nature with three things mined and wrought and coveted by creatures.
2. Possible response: He means that he has turned away from the heroic journey to return home.
3. Students may point out the length of the journeys; how the first has many exciting encounters, while the second is mundane; while the first calls upon Bilbo to take more and more responsibility, while for the second, he is just a co-traveler with Gandalf, etc.
4. Possible response: The blending of the Tookish and Baggins elements of his personality.
5. Possible response: He comes home to discover that he has been declared dead and that having gained treasure in the world, his treasures at home are being sold.
6. Students should recognize that Bilbo has left the heroic realm, and give evidence to support the normalcy and mundane quality of his homecoming.
7. Possible response: He is no longer considered respectable (which would mean that he never went on adventures or did anything unexpected).
8. Possible responses: His Tookish and Baggins sides have melded; he visits with elves; he is more self-assured, etc.
9. Possible response: That the prophecies were correct.
10. Possible response: He finds them hard to believe because he was involved in their fulfillment. Gandalf responds that the things that Bilbo undertook and achieved with support from so many others were hardly managed just for Bilbo's personal growth—they were accomplished for the sake of many and for the fulfillment of the prophecies.

Writer's Forum: Poetry, page 56

Poems will vary. The poem should fit the character for whom it is written.

Writer's Forum: Compare and Contrast a Book and a Movie, page 57

Students should address the questions given for guidance. Facts and opinions should be clearly stated and opinions should be supported by evidence.

Test: Chapters 15–19, page 74

Vocabulary
1. These words are part of the claims made by Bard and Thorin in the parley and aftermath.
2. These words describe the standoff between the elves and men on the one hand and the dwarves on the other hand.
3. These words deal with the interactions of the allies and attackers in the chapter when the goblins and wolves attack.
4. These words tell about the cost of the Battle of Five Armies.
5. These words talk about the rebuilding of Dale and Lake-town following the battle.

Essay Topics
1. Possible responses: Thorin's and/or Gandalf's last words can be taken as thematic. Students should support their interpretations with evidence from the text.

2. Answers will vary. Students may find it entertaining, or be inspired to read the *Lord of the Rings*, or become interested in fantasy as a genre.
3. Answers will vary. Students should support their answers with details from the text.
4. Thorin and Smaug are similar in their avarice and greed, and the gold lust impairs their judgment. They are each in turn King under the Mountain, and their rule isolates them from others. They cannot bear to share their treasure, although they have no need of such wealth, and refer to those who would share it as "thieves." In both cases, the treasure is the cause of their death. The main difference is Thorin's repentance and apology to Bilbo.
5. Answers will vary. Students should explain their responses.
6. Answers will vary. Students may refer to the double theme of Bilbo's interior journey and the journey of the company, and claim that there are multiple themes. Gold lust is certainly important, and many characters' attitudes towards wealth are described.
7. Answers will vary. Many students may agree that this is a good explanation of Gandalf's strong powers of persuasion coupled with his limited powers of action or interference in the course of events.
8. Students may conclude that this book is Bilbo's memoirs.